Kids With Special Needs

Information and Activities to Promote Awareness and Understanding

Writ... ...czal

The Learning Works

Illustrated by

Bev Armstrong

Edited by

Jan Stiles and Kim Clark

Copyright © 1996
The Learning Works, Inc.
P.O. Box 6187
Santa Barbara, California 93160

ISBN: 0-88160-244-2
Library of Congress Number: 95-082093

ACKNOWLEDGMENTS

Contra Costa Child Care Council
Learning Institute
1035 Detroit Ave. Suite 200
Concord, CA 94518

We would like to thank all of the teachers we've had in the past who helped us become what we are today.

We would also like to thank the following medical professionals for taking the time to read and critique the manuscript: Christina Pietrasanta, Director of Communications for the Cystic Fibrosis Foundation in Bethesda, Maryland; May Lee Berry, Regional Cancer Control Director, American Cancer Society, Ventura County (California) Chapter; Dana Butler and Rex Malcolm of the American Heart Association, Greater Los Angeles Affiliate; Elsa Campbell, diabetes support group leader; Dr. Ronald Chochinov (diabetic specialist) of Ventura; Janette Henry-Atkinson, Information and Referral Department, Spina Bifida Association of America, Washington, D.C.; Nancy Smythe, Executive Director, Cleft Palate Foundation, Pittsburgh, Pennsylvania; Dawn S. Marvin, Director of Communications, Asthma and Allergy Foundation of America, Washington, D.C.; Lisa Stockman, Manager of Publications, United Cerebral Palsy Association, Washington, D.C.; Ann Scherer, Director of Communications and Public Relations, Epilepsy Foundation of America, Landover, Maryland; Janet Brown, Project Consultant, National Down Syndrome Society, New York, New York; Veronica M. Zysk, Executive Director, Autism Society of America, Bethesda, Maryland; College Larry Falxa, Instructor for Learning Disabilities and Attention Deficit Disorder, Ventura (California) Community College; Orlene Bowers, Coordinator of Ventura Community College Educational Assistance Center; Florene Bednersh, Ph.D., Director of Special Eduation, Santa Barbara County Education Office; and Len Capozi, Director of Children's Program, The Center for Attitudinal Healing, Sausalito, California.

A special thank you to all of our students, who come to us with many challenges and who have been open to making connections. We appreciate their willingness to try out and help us refine the awareness activities that appear in this book.

Thank you to Loretta Pesetski, who was a wonderful resource person on awareness activities for our manuscript; and to our families, who coped with two couches in the living room, hurried meals, abstract hums for answers, incoherent questions, and general stress management or mismanagement as the case may be.

We would also like to thank the *Ventura Star-News* and photographer Michael Owen Baker for granting us permission to use the cover photo of Eric Ridgeway, "a true athlete who knows no bounds."

CONTENTS

A NOTE TO TEACHERS AND PARENTS

The United States and other countries of the world are becoming increasingly concerned about educational opportunities for children and adults with disabilities. In 1975, the U.S. government passed *Public Law 94-142*, which extended educational rights to school-age children by declaring that all children with disabilities are entitled to a free, appropriate education in the "least restrictive environment" (LRE). As a result of this and other federal laws, children with a variety of disabilities and children without disabilities are having the opportunity to interact and learn together. In 1992, the *Americans with Disabilities Act* was passed, ensuring that adults with disabilities would also have equal access to jobs and education.

The goal of this book is to help teachers, parents, and students explore their feelings, examine their values, discover their own special individuality, and become comfortable with the special needs some students have. *Kids with Special Needs* presents both the myths and the facts about disabilities. Content centers around the following five developmental principles:

- Children notice and ask questions about disabilities.
- Children are able to see their shared abilities and similarities.
- Children need information, words, and support for handling questions about their disabilities.
- Children are curious about the equipment and devices people use for specific disabilities.
- Children may be confused about what a child or adult with a particular disability can and cannot do.

The book's many simulation exercises and learning activities help children gain better insight into what it's like to have a learning or physical disability.

One final note: There has been and continues to be controversy over the correct terms to use in the special education field. This controversy reflects the changing awareness of professionals and advocates for the rights of people with disabilities. In this book, the words "disability" and "disabled" are used because they are the terms currently preferred in the disability rights movement.

People with disabilities are not handicapped by their conditions, but by prejudice, lack of accessibility, and discrimination.

Kids With Special Needs
©1996–The Learning Works

INTRODUCTION

CHAPTER 1:
Living and Working With a Child With Special Needs

CHAPTER 2:
Awareness Activities to Build Empathy and Understanding

CHAPTER 3:
The Brain— A Computer in Charge of Learning

Kids with Special Needs is designed to increase awareness about disabilities in children and the adults who work with them and to promote greater understanding of people who have disabilities. Empathy comes when the learner truly experiences a deep emotional level of understanding.

Kids with Special Needs is divided into eight sections. It is arranged so that activities are open-ended and can be used for a variety of purposes. Teachers and parents should feel free to adapt the activities to the ability level of their children. Much of the material is also suitable for parent education seminars.

The focus of this section is to provide information and to answer questions on the sensitive topics and issues that concern teachers and adults working with children who have special needs. Practical tips for classroom organization are presented along with ideas on creating educational bridges within the school system and links to the community. Hints on preparing information for parent letters or newspapers are also provided.

Parents and teachers all look for immediate and quick solutions to problems or questions that children ask. This section provides practical ideas that help children and adults become aware of individual differences and disabilities. These activities are intended not to be quick fixes, but to serve as thoughtful activities that allow children to develop a deeper understanding of human development and realize an empowering of self. These activities are also suitable for adult workshop presentations.

Acquired head trauma or accidents that damage the brain are becoming more common in our society as children experience the thrills of fast-paced, dare-devil sports and activities. Included in this chapter are activities that start students thinking about learning differences and learning disabilities. All students learn differently, and learning disabilities may appear in many areas, such as spoken language (listening and speaking), written language (reading, writing, and spelling), arithmetic, reasoning, and organizational skills.

Chapter 4:
Communication Disabilities

This chapter covers hearing impairment and disorders of articulation and fluency. It includes classroom curriculum activities to make children aware of the ways sound may be distorted or muffled for people who are hearing impaired.

Chapter 5:
Physical Disabilities

This chapter focuses on impairments related to physical size, visual impairments, certain bodily dysfunctions, and orthopedic disabilities. It includes activities that acquaint children with blindness and the Braille alphabet, and that survey the accessibility of tools and materials in daily life.

Chapter 6:
Facts About Other Health Conditions

This section presents an overview of the health situations and disabling side effects that a teacher will face in a typical classroom. Conditions include AIDS, allergies, arthritis, asthma, birthmarks, burns, cancer, cleft palate, craniofacial deformities, cystic fibrosis, diabetes, skin conditions, and spina bifida. Information on each condition includes a medical definition, the current number of children and adults affected, and general classroom behaviors. Simulation activities, if appropriate, are also provided.

Chapter 7:
Bibliotherapy

The bibliotherapy section is an open-ended application of children's literature to provide insights and understanding in subjects that are sensitive and difficult to talk about. Reading the appropriate book at the right time can provide an introduction to a sensitive topic or issue. Books are listed by specific disability. Annotated entries are provided.

Chapter 8:
Resources and Organizations of Interest

Books, films, videos, and computer resources are listed, along with the primary organizations that offer unique materials for the disabled. An extensive listing of 800 phone numbers is also provided.

This book is unique. Its activities are appropriate for young children and for adults who wish to develop a background on disabilities. The book also can be used as a supplemental text for seminars and workshops addressing issues facing people with disabilities.

Many states now require teachers to take a course that covers mainstreaming and disabilities. This book serves well as a supplemental text for a course that examines education in the least restrictive environment. It provides "hands-on" experiences to simulate each disability.

CHAPTER 1
LIVING AND WORKING WITH A
CHILD WITH SPECIAL NEEDS

INTRODUCTION

Adults working with children need to get in touch with their feelings about children with disabilities. This section helps teachers and adults working with children explore their own attitudes, and it provides information about the legal mandates for education. Because children pick up negative connotations about disabilities from adults, it is important to address the following:

- It is often difficult not to react negatively to people who are different from us because we do not understand them and what they have experienced.

- Physical beauty is important in our culture, so we feel uncomfortable around those whose appearance does not meet cultural ideals.

- Some adults and children feel guilty about being able bodied when they are around people with disabilities.

- Adults feel vulnerable around persons with disabilities because they are reminded that they, too, could become disabled. Young children may even believe that disabilities are contagious.

- Many disabilities have been used as symbols for evil in the media: hunchbacks, arms with hooks, peg legs, and eye patches.

The Success Cycle

All human beings have basic needs, such as food, shelter, and clothing. After these basic needs are met, the need for security is most crucial. Security is central to the cycle of success, a cycle where supportive behaviors lead to improved self-concept, greater motivation, and higher achievement and function. This cycle opens the channels to understanding and to recognizing the personal worth of every individual. It helps all children, not only those with disabilities, to become comfortable with who and what they are.

All of us need to feel empowered — to have a basic feeling of control and security in our lives and to feel confident about who we are, what we know, and what we can do. We need to be respected for who we are as individuals and for where we are in our personal journeys as professionals and/or parents living and maturing with children with special needs. We need a safe place in which to ask questions, share difficult feelings, and make mistakes. Children, too, need a supportive environment that fosters growth, self-worth, and accomplishment.

Take time to think about the cycle of success. It starts with a supportive relationship. Using the cycle with learners of all ages builds empathy and understanding.

THE GRIEF CYCLE

For most, the miracle of birth is a joyful occasion when a child is welcomed into a world of opportunities. For some families, however, birth may be a time for tears, despair, confusion, and fear. It may demand a totally new life style for all involved, a life full of mysterious, frightening, and unique problems to solve.

When children are born with disabilities, their families go through a grieving process. Most parents, upon learning that their child has a disability, react initially with feelings of astonishment and shock. Before they can accept the truth of the situation, they must work through a normal series of emotional reactions. These reactions are called the grief cycle. When a child, young adult, or mature adult is faced with a newly acquired disability or health condition, the same stages of grief must be resolved for the person to cope with the situation and accept it as it is.

There are five major attitudinal stages in the grief cycle that most individuals or parents go through when they realize that their child has a disability or that they themselves have one.

Remember . . .
- The attitudinal stages do not always occur in sequence.
- Stages may be repeated and may overlap other stages.
- Each stage must run its course until the next emerges.
- The degree of emotional response, intense to mild, varies widely between parents and among family members and friends.
- These stages are common to all individuals and are not influenced by a person's bank account or intelligence.
- It is not possible to be counseled out of one stage into another; the individual goes at his or her own rate.

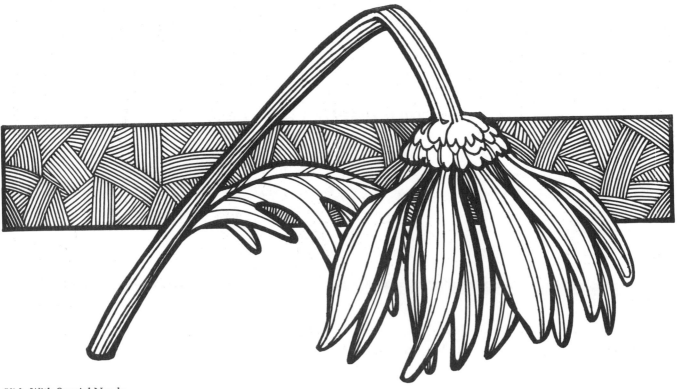

THE GRIEF CYCLE

Stage 1: Denial and Isolation

Initially, individuals experience a sense of shock or disbelief about their particular circumstance. They often seek further medical evaluations with the hope that the previous diagnosis was in error. Parents may say, "No, this can't be true; there must be a mistake." This denial functions as a buffer or defense mechanism to protect people from the pain of unexpected bad news. This stage is characterized by an overwhelming need to maintain a sense of optimism and hopefulness.

Stage 2: Anger

After denial is faced, it is replaced with rage, anger, envy, and resentment. The question adults ask themselves is, "Why me?" The anger is often displaced in every direction and may be projected randomly toward others. Newly disabled adults often alienate friends and professionals with their expressions of displaced anger and rage. During this stage, there is an unrelenting feeling of persecution that often gets expressed in the form of hostile blame or excessive demands made on others.

Stage 3: Bargaining

At this stage, there is hope that "good behavior" or a commitment to a special service or organization may bring about a spontaneous remission or cure. Many times, these bargains are made secretly with God, with the promise of good behavior or a life dedicated to helping others in exchange for a healing.

Stage 4: Depression

When the numbness wears off, rage and anger are replaced with a sense of loss and depression. The loss may be perceived in many ways: loss of a rosy future for the child, loss of a job, loss of personal independence, loss of self-esteem, or the loss of value as a parent. The impact of changing life roles and responsibilities adds to the sense of loss.

Depression is seen most quickly in the child's or adult's bodily functions. Common signs are changes in sleep, loss of or increase in appetite, and decreased mental functioning. Common feelings include helplessness, hopelessness, and worthlessness. At this stage adults become high risks for suicide, and the potential for serious injury must be assessed.

Stage 5: Acceptance

Given time and support while working through the previous stages, a child or an adult will be able to accept his or her new fate without being depressed or angry. Having had the opportunity to express envy of a healthy body and to mourn the loss of so many meaningful activities, the individual will be able to face reality with a sense of positive adjustment and expectation.

A POSITIVE EXPERIENCE

A positive attitude is critical in dealing with a disability. Most youngsters with disabilities can lead full lives. Their parents' lives can also be enriched by the challenge of raising a child with special needs and acquiring the unique parenting skills that the task requires. Parental attitudes toward a child's disability set the stage for how the child develops. To maintain a constructive attitude toward their child with special needs, parents must have . . .

- emotional support from each other and other parents and from organizations; community agencies; or private, individual, or group counseling services.
- information and results regarding all tests and assessments.
- knowledge about the causes of the disability, the diagnosis, and the prognosis.
- positive intervention programs: therapy, infant stimulation, schooling, classes for parents, and additional resources for information and research.

Parents can learn to think positively if they . . .
- rethink assumptions about disabled persons.
- reassess their values regarding what is important in life.
- learn to look at the disabled child's total growth and special gifts.
- learn the best ways to meet the special needs of the child within the family structure.
- continue to adjust to unique situations and to grow as parents.

WHERE DO YOU START?

Once parents reach the point of accepting the situation and accepting their child, the quest for knowledge begins. One or both parents will become detectives looking for programs to help their child. Ultimately, most parents become experts on their child's disability. Today, many resources exist to help these parent detectives in their search for knowledge, solutions, and support.

Start closest to home.

If you are one of these detectives, begin by calling your local school district and asking for the special education office or department. Before you call, jot down your questions and the types of information or assistance you are seeking. Listen carefully to the responses. Ask to have printed information mailed to you. Keep a log of organizations and individuals you have contacted and a record of the results of each contact.

Use 800 phone numbers.

Through the combined efforts of people with disabilities, their parents, teachers, professionals, and various funding sources, many organizations, foundations, and resource agencies have been established to educate the general population. Their 800 telephone numbers, plus other key organizations and resources, are listed on pages 185 to 187. Call and ask to have information mailed to you.

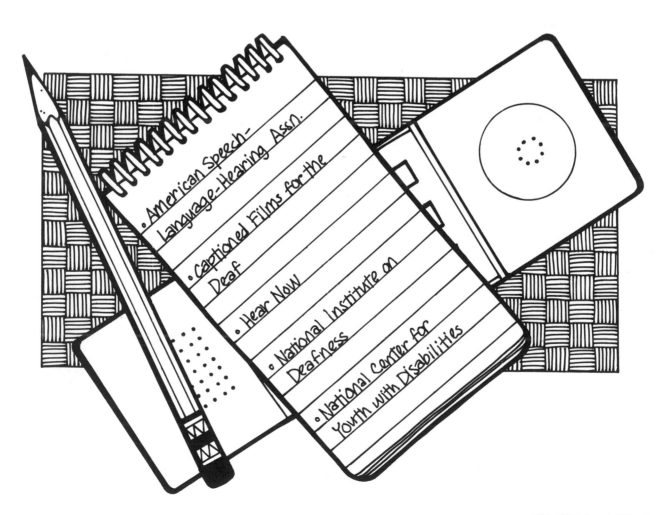

WHERE DO YOU START?

Get referrals.

Often an 800 number is established so an organization can refer callers to local support groups. Support groups are usually found at the state level and in major cities. Keep calling until you find the right resource and assistance.

Join support groups.

Every member has a special story to tell and has gained knowledge or strength by living through difficult experiences. Sharing these stories is part of the healing process, part of the advocate process, and, most of all, part of the process that provides physical, mental, or emotional support for parents.

Volunteer and participate in advocacy opportunities.

As your child progresses through his or her school years, you will accumulate valuable information to pass along to other parents "new" to the field of disability awareness. Volunteer your services and take an active role in promoting and enhancing the quality of life of all individuals with disabilities — whether children or adults.

SPECIAL NEEDS LEGISLATION

What is Public Law 94-142?

Across the nation, school personnel, school boards, teachers, and parents are grappling with complicated issues of how best to educate all children — not just children with special needs. When legislation is enacted into law, compliance becomes a critical point for all individuals concerned. In many states, court cases involving children with disabilities are waiting to be tried. In 1975, the United States government passed Public Law 94-142, also referred to as P. L. 94-142, which extends educational rights to school-age children. The law declares that all children with disabilities are entitled to a free, appropriate education in the least restrictive environment. The law states:

> "Each public agency shall insure: That to the maximum extent appropriate, handicapped children . . . are educated with children who are not handicapped," and that children will be segregated "only when the nature or severity of the handicap is such that regular classes with the use of supplementary aids and services cannot be achieved satisfactorily."

What is IDEA?

IDEA is an acronym for public law 101-476, the Individuals with Disabilities Act of 1990. This law updated and added to Public Law 92-142. The passage of this legislation:

- changed the language of the law to read "disability" in place of "handicap."
- defined support services as "assistive technology devices" and "assistive technology services."
- provided funding to attract and recruit persons from diverse groups into special education careers.
- added autism and traumatic brain injury (TBI) to the list of disabilities covered under the law and mandated a study of the condition commonly known as attention deficit disorder.
- required that IEPs address needed transition services for all students, but specifically those age 16 and older.

Other important legislation

Two other pieces of legislation—the Vocational Rehabilitation Act of 1973 and the Americans with Disabilities Act of 1990 (Public Law 101-336)—also address the needs of individuals with disabilities. Section 504 of the Vocational Rehabilitation Act of 1973 provides for a free, appropriate public education for school-aged children with disabilities and forbids discrimination in employment, in admissions to institutions of higher education, and in the provision of health, welfare, and other social services.

The ADA or Americans with Disabilities Act of 1990 is a comprehensive law designed to "provide a clear and comprehensive national mandate for the elimination of discrimination against individuals with disabilities." This law is being enforced and is responsible for increased employment of individuals with disabilities and increased access to public facilities such as restaurants, hotels, theaters, offices, and public transportation services.

This legislation introduced new terminology that teachers and parents need to become familiar with and understand. Because services and options vary somewhat across the nation, a good place to begin seeking information is the local school district office. Most will provide printed copies of the laws and materials describing services available.

WHAT DO "MAINSTREAMING" AND "INCLUSION" MEAN?

Mainstreaming refers to the process of integrating students with disabilities into the regular classrooms and providing concrete assistance for the classroom teacher (non-special education teachers). The mainstreaming process allows the child with special needs to be a member of a regular classroom with supplemental resources or services provided as needed. In some instances, the child is moved from special classes into a regular classroom for part of the instructional day.

Inclusion is a newer term that is sometimes used to describe the mainstreaming process. Advocates of "full inclusion" maintain that the general education classroom is the most appropriate full-time placement for all students with disabilities, not just those students with mild learning or behavior problems. In the full inclusion model, students do not leave the main classroom to receive additional instruction or services; instead, the support services are provided within the regular classroom setting.

What Is Education in the Least Restrictive Environment?

Education in the least restrictive environment means that a student must be allowed to participate in as much of the general education program as is appropriate in view of his or her educational needs. In other words, no child should be separated from students without disabilities any more than is educationally necessary. Also, a child's program should be located as close to home as possible, meaning that program options at his or her neighborhood school should be considered first.

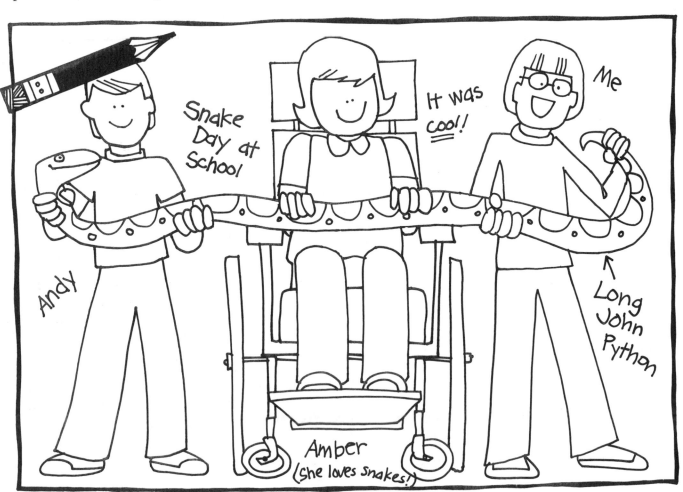

WHAT IS AN IEP?

An IEP is an *Individualized Educational Program* that has been specially designed for any student eligible for special education. A child who has been identified as having special needs must be assessed to determine the nature and extent of his or her needs in order to create the optimal learning environment. A range of specialists, which may include a psychologist, social worker, speech and language specialist, interpreters, and therapists, meet with an administrator, the classroom teacher, parent(s) or legal guardian(s), and, if appropriate, the student, to help determine the child's needs and plan the appropriate educational strategies and environment.

Before an IEP meeting, the facilitator or program specialist in charge will do the following:
- Select individuals to serve on the IEP team.
- Arrange a meeting date and time, invite the parents, and send confirmation and reminder notices.
- Assemble the required and pertinent information on the child.

What Happens at an IEP Conference or Meeting?

- Introductions identify each person there, giving the person's position and reason for attending. Parents are made to feel welcome, and an approximate time frame is established for the meeting.

- The purpose of the meeting is stated and includes the following: review of assessment data, student eligibility criteria for special education, development of goals and objectives based on identified needs, and a decision for appropriate program placement to best meet the child's needs.

- Before the conference concludes, forms are completed and signed; educational goals and objectives for the student are stated in writing. The rights of parents and child are summarized, and a time for review (within one year) is scheduled. Parents are informed of their right to request a review at any time if concerns arise regarding the appropriateness of the IEP and/or placement.

SPECIAL EDUCATION TIME LINE

P. L. 94-142 mandates a series of steps that must be taken before a child with special needs can receive services. The following steps and terminology are described and outlined for the adult unfamiliar with the process.

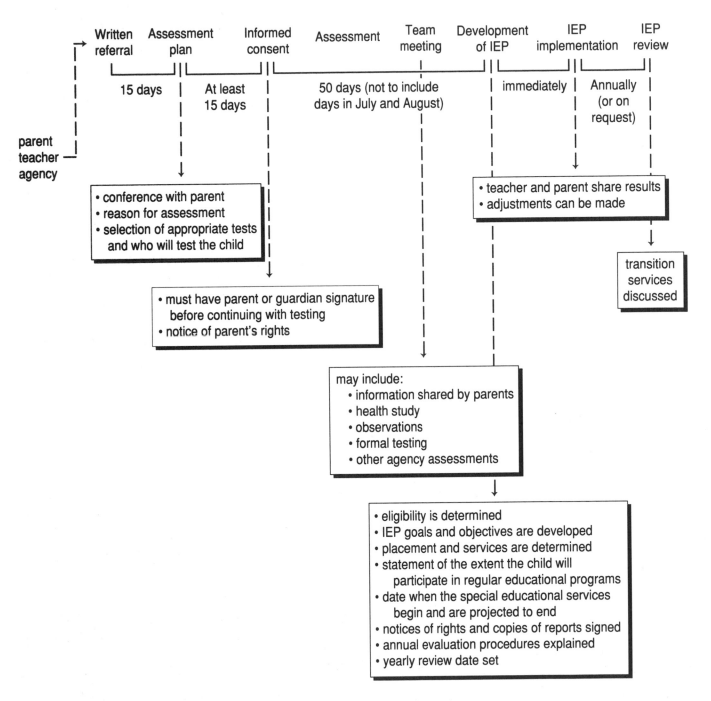

Note: IEPs must be developed within 50 days after the parents' consent to the assessment plan, not counting days between the regular school session or term, or days of school vacation in excess of five days.

WHAT PROGRAMS ARE AVAILABLE?

During an IEP meeting, program and placement options may be discussed. The following are descriptions of typical program structures across the nation.

Early Intervention Program

This program is designed to provide early intervention services to infants and toddlers (birth to age three) who have special needs. The program is divided into two classes: birth to eighteen months, and eighteen to thirty-six months. The classes, usually housed in a publicly owned building or at a school site, emphasize student/parent training. Other aspects of this program include home visits, a parent support group, and family involvement activities.

Preschool Programs

Preschool children with special needs may be served in several ways. School districts may have special classes with designated instruction and services. Head Start, a federally funded program, has designated instruction and services if the family qualifies. A private preschool, with tuition paid by the parent, may have accommodations for children with special needs.

Regular Class Program

A student with special needs may be placed in a regular classroom program when an IEP team determines that the child's needs can be met in that setting with the use of supplementary aids and services. Often, volunteers or special teaching aides paid by the county or district will be assigned to work with the child. This provides one-on-one assistance for the child.

Resource Specialist Program (RSP)

The RSP is designed to provide special education instruction and services for students with special needs who are assigned to a regular classroom for most of the instructional day. Responsibilities of the RSP teacher include providing instruction, monitoring pupil progress, revising IEPs, and coordinating services and appointments with parents and staff.

Designated Instruction and Services (DIS)

This type of service includes, but is not limited to, the following: speech and language remediation, audiological services, orientation and mobility instruction, instruction in the home or hospital, adapted physical education, physical and occupational therapy, vision services, specialized driver training instruction, counseling and guidance, psychological services other than assessment and development of the IEP, parent counseling, health and nursing services, social worker assistance, vocational education and career development, recreational services, and specialized services for low-incidence disabilities.

WHAT PROGRAMS ARE AVAILABLE?

Special Classes and Centers

A student may be eligible for a special class when the IEP team determines that his or her educational needs cannot be met satisfactorily by attendance in regular classes for the majority of the school day, even with the use of supplemental aids and services. Students in special classes will participate in nonacademic and extracurricular services and activities with their nondisabled peers to the maximum extent appropriate.

Private, Nonsectarian School Services

This placement is considered only when a student's needs cannot be met within public school programs.

State Special Schools

This placement is an option only when no appropriate placement is available and when a residential placement is needed for the child to meet his or her educational goals.

State Hospital Facility

A special education program for a student residing in a local state hospital may be an option if an appropriate program exists.

Other

Special education instruction may also occur in settings other than the classroom. Specially designed instruction that meets the needs of the student can take place in a variety of locations and situations.

Basic Assumptions

1. Special education is a service provided to individuals, not a program placement.
2. Services and placement options are determined by the individualized-education program team.
3. Families are integral and fully participating members of the IEP team.
4. Services are offered throughout an array of placement options.
5. Some of the options that may be offered are inclusive education, residential school, special day class, etc.

COMMON QUESTIONS ADULTS ASK ABOUT KIDS WITH SPECIAL NEEDS

"I don't have any experience in caring for a child with a disability. Will I be able to handle it?"

Most teachers and child care facilitators are very capable of working with and caring for children with disabilities. The skills required are typically the same skills needed to nurture any child. The primary ingredients in providing quality care to children with special needs are observation skills, a willingness and desire to be flexible, and an openness to learn from each child, the family, and the support team of specialists.

"Do all children with disabilities require intensive, individual care?"

The answer lies with each child and the special needs of that child. Generally, since the abilities of each child vary, so will the amount of individual attention. Some children will be able to participate in all activities, with only minor changes. Some children will require adult assistance in most activities.

"Will I need to protect the child with disabilities from being hurt during play with other children in the class?"

All of the children in the class need to have adequate precautions taken for their safety, including the child with a disability. The child with a disability does **not** need to be protected from trying new things or from making friends. Whether a child becomes a successful learner or experiences failure depends on the teacher or adult facilitator. All children need to learn to be independent. They need to experience feelings of celebration for the successful completion of tasks and to learn ways to cope with the failures that all children experience.

"Will I have to change my whole routine to accommodate a child with a disability?"

Any child with a disability enjoys and learns from the same activities that benefit all children. Children with special needs like to create, play with blocks, and play outdoors. Depending on the severity of the condition, some or all activities may have to be adapted to make them easier for the child. A small number of children will be totally dependent on adults for assistance in activities.

"How can I find out more about disabilities?"

Educate yourself. Conferences, workshops, and educational journals provide information on special needs. Read a book or rent a videotape. Many books and movies provide personal accounts of living with a disability. A suggested list of journals, books, and videos is provided in Chapter 8: Resources and Organizations of Interest. A list of toll-free numbers for organizations that will give you information on disabilities is also provided. The local child care resource and referral agency or your local school district can also give you information and a list of resources.

COMMON QUESTIONS ADULTS ASK ABOUT KIDS WITH SPECIAL NEEDS

"Where can I go for help?"

Parents of a child with a disability are usually a great resource for the classroom teacher. Special education teachers, therapists, and public health nurses are valuable sources for information, assistance, support, and suggestions. Teachers checking with local medical resources will discover that members of the medical profession are willing to explain a child's disability to teachers or care providers. Check with the local child care resource and referral agency for training opportunities.

"What kinds of questions can I expect from the other children in the class?"

Children will ask questions that are specific to their interests and age level. One of the foremost concerns children have is, "Can I catch what you have?" Teachers can expect a range of questions on food preferences, TV programs, play activities, and hobbies, plus questions on physical routines like getting dressed, going to the bathroom, and taking a bath. Responses to questions need to be open and honest and to reflect that the child with the disability has the same kind of heart, thinks the same way, and wants to accomplish the same goals and participate in the same activities as all children, even though the activities may be completed in a different fashion and/or with assistance.

Questions Children May Ask
- How did that person get that way?
- Can I catch what he or she has?
- Why doesn't that person's body work right?
- Why does that person look funny?
- How come he or she has to miss so much school?
- Will he or she die?

Guidelines for Responding
1. Be sure you understand the question the child is asking.
2. Always correct misinformation or incorrect assumptions.
3. Don't ignore children's fears; address them.
4. Respond immediately to a question, fear, or inaccurate information.
5. Examine your own behavior and language.

Teachable moments are life's serendipity! Be prepared! Teachable moments are unplanned, spontaneous events for parents and teachers to anticipate with zest. These moments are powerful teaching tools. Enjoy, value, and savor each one.

STEPS TO IMPLEMENTING DISABILITY AWARENESS IN THE CLASSROOM

1. **Gather visual materials for displays, bulletin boards, and learning games.**
   Collect photos, newspaper clippings, greeting cards, posters, magazine cutouts, and advertisements that reflect a wide range of special needs. These materials can be used on bulletin boards and in posters or other displays or demonstrations to increase the level of visual awareness of disabilities.

Recommendation: Find a parent or volunteer to assist you in this time-consuming process, or adopt an upper-grade classroom that will collaborate with your class on this project. Specific tasks can include the following:
   - Spend time cutting illustrations and photos from magazines and other publications.
   - Call the 800 numbers listed on page 185-187 and request information.
   - Write to request free catalogues from publishers and video companies.
   - Search thrift stores and garage sales for props to use in dramatic play.

2. **Gradually add visual materials to your classroom.**
   Take note of how children and parents respond.

Recommendation: You may want to send a letter to parents explaining that special needs awareness will be a focus for your class. You could request help in finding materials and ask parents to note the comments their children make at home.

3. **Create new interest areas in the classroom to reflect disability awareness.**

Recommendation: Set up various role-playing situations using crutches, wheelchairs, and other adaptive devices.

Kids With Special Needs
©1996–The Learning Works

STEPS TO IMPLEMENTING DISABILITY AWARENESS IN THE CLASSROOM

4. Develop small and large group activities.

You might plan field trips, arrange for guest speakers from local organizations, and invite individuals with special needs to spend time in your classroom.

Recommendation: Ideas and suggestions throughout the book will help you locate and choose a variety of speakers within your local community. See the activity descriptions and guidelines for interviews, located under "Guest Speakers" in Chapter 2: Awareness Activities to Build Empathy and Understanding.

5. Use daily events and experiences as opportunities to talk with children informally about special needs.

Opportunities include ideas, issues, or questions children raise during casual interactions such as arrival, departure, mealtime, nap time, and free play.

Recommendation: Each week, read a book selected from the bibliotherapy list and incorporate that information into casual conversations with children. Call the archives department of your local newspaper for copies of stories they have printed on students with disabilities and volunteers. Read or discuss these news stories with your class.

6. Point out children's biased remarks and behaviors as they occur in the classroom.

Ideally, you will feel comfortable enough to respond to a child's direct question or comment openly and honestly. These situations are the most difficult for teachers to deal with because they catch teachers off guard.

7. Incorporate special needs awareness into the curriculum.

Begin by using the ideas and activities in this book. Then adapt the ideas or try out new ones to meet the specific needs of your students.

HOME AND CLASSROOM ENVIRONMENT

When organizing and preparing an environment for children with disabilities, it is important to keep the following details in mind. It is also important that teachers and parents exchange thoughts and information on the following considerations.

Fatigue

Children with special needs may experience a fading of energy at specific periods of the day or as a side effect of medication. Observe each child's pattern and adjust the activity schedule.

Health Problems

Certain types of disabilities have health alerts that accompany them, such as a child with cancer being vulnerable to common childhood diseases. School districts have schedules and guidelines for dispensing medication. Contact the parents and physicians for information.

Specific Learning Difficulties

The special education department of your local public school district or support agencies may provide assessments of the child's specific problem learning areas. Tailor the instructional day to meet those suggestions and observe the child's progress closely.

Lack of Environmental Organization

Depending upon the disability, changes may need to be made within the physical classroom or home layout and room arrangement. Think about all the areas that the child with a disability would like to access and remove as many barriers as possible. The flow of traffic within the classroom is a key ingredient to eliminating frustration.

Anxiety

Every child and adult wishes to present a positive image to the world and may outwardly appear to do so with courage. Inside, however, feelings of anxiety may be overwhelming. Ask the person with a disability about specific concerns he or she has before that person enters the new educational environment.

Embarrassment in Front of Peers

Make daily life as smooth as possible. There will be awkward moments with the beginning of new relationships. Ask the parents of the child for any tips about preventing embarrassing situations.

Excessive TV

Avoid using television as a baby-sitter at home or in the educational setting. Control the amount of time any child spends watching TV and monitor the programs for appropriate viewing content.

SPECIAL NEEDS CHECKLIST

This checklist offers tips for arranging the learning environment for the child with special needs. It is important to set the stage for learning so that the child is comfortable and relaxed.

☐ *Prepare a learning environment at home and at school.*
- Have clear and predictable rules
- Make schedules flexible, yet structured; provide a regular routine.
- Use feedback and logical consequences.
- Limit distractions.
- Schedule activities for success.
- Use clearly worded cues.

☐ *Optimize all organizational aspects of the learning environment.*
- Provide resources and areas that promote good work habits.
- Organize and complete paperwork.
- Schedule discussion times and work periods.

☐ *Use attention-keeping behaviors.*
- Prepare the child for transitions.
- Engage the child's attention.
- Clarify what needs attention.
- Respond to and follow the child's lead.

☐ *Pace learning and activity changes.*
- Develop schedules appropriate for the age level.
- Provide active versus quiet time.
- Include indoor and outdoor activities.
- Balance teacher-directed and child-chosen activities.

☐ *Create a physical environment that is barrier free.*
- Make sure the traffic pattern flows smoothly.
- Arrange an access room where needed.
- Be sure there are bathroom facilities nearby.
- Provide a variety of textures and surfaces.
- Observe safety precautions.

☐ *Be a role model in your teaching.*
- Talk through events and expectations.
- Promote calmness and coping skills.
- Promote independence.
- Use hands-on activities.

☐ *Locate and use paths to information.*
- Contact the special education department for suggestions.
- Talk to the principal about school adaptations.
- Discuss ways to share information through parent letters or news releases.
- Become more aware of family situations and siblings.

SHARING INFORMATION

Let the public know the types of activities that are going on in your classroom. This is a great way to let your students know they are doing a great job and to advocate awareness and empathy for kids with disabilities. Parents, too, like to be informed about what is happening in the classroom.

News Releases

When preparing information about classroom activities to share with a local publication, such as a newspaper or newsletter, do the following:

- Type on 8½" x 11" nonerasable paper or use a computer. School letterhead is preferred. Always state the name of the author/contact person in the upper left corner of the paper. Include a phone number where you can be reached if questions arise.
- Leave wide margins and double space your information.
- Limit your information to one page whenever possible. Make it newsworthy and interesting.
- Be sure that the information is accurate. Always answer who, what, where, when, and why.
- Include the release date—the day you would like the article to appear in the paper.
- Have another person proofread the article to catch mistakes and to make sure the copy is accurate.

Informative Letter

Teachers may feel that parents of nondisabled children need to be informed about a child with special needs. Here is a sample letter concerning a classmate with cancer. Be sure to get permission from the student's parents beforehand.

School Letterhead

Date

Dear Parents,

This year our class will have a unique opportunity to learn more about a disability that affects hundreds of young children each year. (Name of child) has recently joined our (grade level) grade class. (He/She) has been diagnosed as having cancer and at the present time is in remission and doing well.

I want to assure you that this disease is **not contagious**. (Name of child)'s cancer is being controlled by chemotherapy, which kills the cancer cells in the blood but also kills some of the normal cells. When normal cells die, there can be a problem of lowered immunity, which means it is more difficult to fight infection, especially a virus infection such as chickenpox.

If (name of child) were to contract any childhood illness, it could be serious. If he/she has been exposed, the doctors will give medicine to lessen the effects. Please let us know as soon as possible if your child is absent due to a viral infection.

Sincerely,
Classroom Teacher
School phone number

VOLUNTEERS ARE GREAT!

Children need to see community members working together to create a better world. There are certain to be many volunteers in your neighborhood who would be happy to share their experiences with the class.

A few examples:
- Canines for Independence or Guide Dogs for the Blind
- Heads Up — horseback riding experiences for those with disabilities
- Monkey Helpers — monkeys trained to assist those with physical limitations
- Facilitated therapy with pets
- Hobbies — stamp and coin collecting, arts and craft activities
- Resident dog and animal programs
- Readers that visit classrooms to share uplifting stories about children with special needs
- Musical groups comprised of musicians and singers with disabilities
- Theater groups with actors and support personnel with disabilities

Check local service clubs for volunteers to assist in your classroom. The more adults with positive attitudes that you have working with kids, the greater the children's involvement and participation.

Investigate which groups might have the resources and experience to make school assembly presentations.

If students in the class are old enough, they may decide to become volunteers themselves in one of the worthy projects listed above. Check out each organization thoroughly before encouraging or approving participation by students. Find out the insurance considerations, standards for training, length of training, physical demands of the volunteer position, and any other important considerations.

RESOURCE LIST

Use a phone book to fill in the phone number for the agencies and organizations listed below. This will provide you with a handy reference sheet that applies directly to your community.

Local School District

_____

_____

Special Education Services

_____

Contact person: _____

_____

State Department of Education _____

_____

_____

State Commission for the Blind

_____

Department of Health and Human Services

_____

Mayor's Office _____

City Council Representatives

_____

_____

_____

_____

State Senator(s) _____

State Representative _____

U.S. Senator(s) _____

_____

U.S. Representative(s) _____

Child Support Program_____

_____

Disabled or Handicapped Services

_____

Family Social Services _____

_____

Home Medical Support Services

_____

Hospitals_____

_____

Legal Service for Persons with Disabilities

_____

Mental Health Services_____

Poison Control Center_____

Nursing Homes _____

Rehabilitation Centers _____

_____

_____

School Volunteer Program _____

Social Service Organizations _____

_____

Speech/Hearing Centers _____

_____

State Bar Association _____

Transportation for the Disabled

_____

_____

Other Special Community Services

_____

_____

American Cancer Society _____

American Diabetes Association _____

_____

American Association for Retired Persons

_____

American Red Cross_____

Arthritis Foundation _____

Cystic Fibrosis Center _____

Down Syndrome Association _____

Easter Seal Society _____

March of Dimes _____

Mental Health Association _____

Muscular Dystrophy Association

_____

Retired Senior Volunteer Program

_____

United Cerebral Palsy_____

United Way _____

Other_____

CHAPTER 2
AWARENESS ACTIVITIES TO BUILD EMPATHY AND UNDERSTANDING

INTRODUCTION

The following collection of activities will provide the teacher or parent with ways to help children and adults gain a wider perspective of what it is like to be disabled in today's world. By using the activities in this section to create opportunities for children to experience the feelings of people with disabilities, those parents, teachers, and adults who work with children can play an important part in reducing misinformation about disabilities.

To make this section of the book relevant and timely, you may want to consider the following four suggestions:

- You do not need to move consecutively through the activities presented. Each activity addresses a different condition or situation, and the order of use should be based on your understanding of your students' needs.

- The activities are written for students, preschool through adult, and may need to be adapted slightly to be totally effective.

- Whenever children are asked to express opinions or feelings, an element of risk is involved. An atmosphere of warmth and unconditional trust without judgment is crucial when asking children to share personal impressions and viewpoints.

- Make sure you allow enough time for discussion at the end of each activity. It is important that children have an opportunity for a "debriefing" so they are not left with unresolved questions, feelings, or misunderstandings.

Remember, each of these activities will foster greater empathy and understanding for the disabled. Change is not easy, but through our classroom efforts, we can guide children toward shaping a society that offers acceptance for everyone.

A CLASS SURVEY

WHAT YOU DO

For each statement below, check the box that best describes how you feel.

Important: There are no right or wrong answers! Just think about how you feel. Then answer honestly.

	YES	NO	MAYBE
1. I feel okay around people who have disabilities.	❑	❑	❑
2. I think people with disabilities should live and work with everybody else.	❑	❑	❑
3. I have seen people with disabilities who are employed at a local business.	❑	❑	❑
4. People with disabilities are able to ride bicycles, drive cars, and participate in sports.	❑	❑	❑
5. A person who has a disability can marry a person who does not have a disability.	❑	❑	❑
6. People who have disabilities can be good parents.	❑	❑	❑
7. Kids who have disabilities should go to the same schools as everyone else.	❑	❑	❑
8. Kids who have disabilities can be just as smart as those who do not have disabilities.	❑	❑	❑
9. Kids who have disabilities can have many friends.	❑	❑	❑
10. I would like to make friends with someone who has a disability.	❑	❑	❑
11. During recess on the school playground, I would play with kids who have disabilities.	❑	❑	❑
12. I would invite someone who has a disability over to my house to play.	❑	❑	❑
13. Kids who have disabilities are the same in many ways as those who do not.	❑	❑	❑
14. Kids who have disabilities can be as happy as those who do not have disabilities.	❑	❑	❑
15. Kids who have disabilities can live on their own when they grow up.	❑	❑	❑

• Bring in newspaper or magazine articles that support your point of view about disabilities. Share the articles with your class.

Kids With Special Needs
©1996–The Learning Works

MAKING NEW FRIENDS

Everybody has favorite activities. Using the list below, ask each child to create a poster of favorite things. Possible poster titles might be *My Favorite Things* or *All About Me*. Help younger children label their posters.

Then try to find a group of children with special needs who will do this same activity. Arrange for both groups to exchange drawings and class photos. Allow children to examine one another's drawings to find things in common. The goal of this activity is to get past the disability and look at the person.

My Favorite Things

To enhance comparison, you can have all children include the same categories on their posters. To do that, provide a list like the following:

color	food
game	sport
TV show	song, book, or poem
animal or pet	holiday
time of day	season
amusement park	place to visit

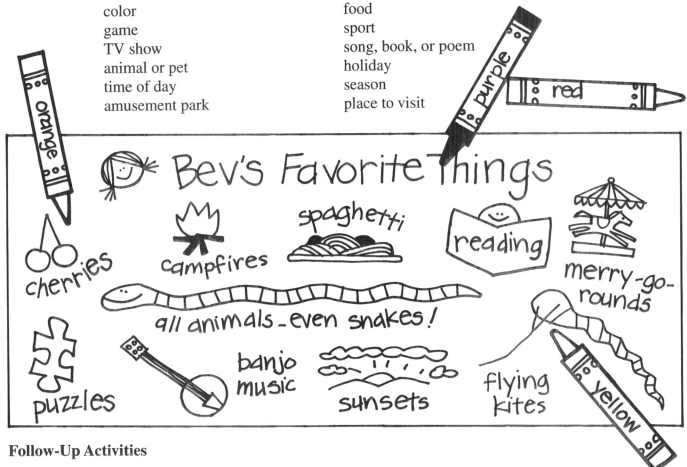

Follow-Up Activities

1. Visit the class of students with special needs and meet the children who made the posters.

2. Plan a joint outing to a local park or picnic area. Ask children to wear their favorite colors and bring their favorite stuffed animal, toy, food, etc. Organize and play games that are suitable for both groups of children.

3. Set up a pen-pal exchange between the classes. Have students exchange letters or class videos. Videotape each class doing its favorite group activities and then film each child holding his or her poster.

AWARENESS ACTIVITY: WHAT IS A DISABILITY?

The following experience helps older students and adults understand the general stereotypes associated with the word *disability*. This activity serves well as both an introductory and a culminating activity since it gives participants an opportunity to express new insights toward people with disabilities as individuals.

1. Define the word *disability*.

Divide the large group into smaller groups of five to six students. Hand out marking pens and large sheets of newsprint. Ask each group to define the word *disability*. Then post the definitions on the walls with tape or write them on a blackboard, white board, or overhead acetate.

2. Find your category.

Call the group to order and state the following:

> "It's great to see such a large group of nondisabled people here today. At this time, I would like to assign each of you to a specific group. Notice the cards posted on the walls and labeled with the numbers 1 through 10. When I read a statement that fits you, please go stand by the number for that statement."

Read ten statements that categorize those participating. Choose from the list below and/or make up your own statements to fit the group. Be sure to include at least one statement that targets people who qualify for more than one category.

Possible statements:

Everyone who is wearing glasses or contacts, move to Position 1.
Everyone who is left-handed, please move to Position 2.
Everyone who does not know how to swim, proceed to 3.
Everyone who isn't bilingual, please go to Position 4.
Everyone who owns a computer and is proficient in its use, go to Position 5.
Everyone who has a college degree, go to 6.
Anyone who meets more than two criteria already listed, go to Position 7.

Continue in this manner until you have 10 statements. The object is to find statements that define one characteristic that makes an individual different from the majority of the group.

3. Consider your feelings.

Ask participants to think about their feelings and reactions to being categorized. Then reassemble the large group. Lead a discussion using questions such as:

- Do you still want to keep the definition of disabled that you made up earlier?
- How many of you "normal" individuals were disabled according to our new definitions?
- How many of you feel that you fit into more than one group and thus had multiple disabilities?

FIELD TRIPS

Field trips are a valuable hands-on learning experience for a class studying a specific disability. Look in the local phone book for the nearest field trip site.

When you call, ask about . . .

location — Get the address and request a map and/or directions.

time and date — Confirm the scheduling.

contact person — Find out who will be your guide at the field trip site.

parking — Ask about parking areas or facilities at the site.

Before you go, be sure to . . .

make transportation arrangements.

notify parents and get any needed permissions.

orient the children by having pre- and post-trip discussions.

arrange for adults to help with supervision.

take safety precautions and go over do's and don'ts with the school group.

make a plan for emergencies.

Phone Book Listings for Possible Field Trip Sites

Ambulance service (non-emergency)

Audiology center

Automobile hand and foot controls

Community speech and hearing centers

Drug stores with a line of medical equipment for people with disabilities

Handicapped and disabled services

Hearing aid repair facilities

Local hospital rehabilitation or physical therapy departments

Occupational therapists

Ophthalmologists

Opticians

Optometrists

Physical therapists

Podiatrists

Prosthetic devices

Schools, both academic and special education

Social service organizations

Speech and language pathologists

Telecommunications equipment for the disabled

Van conversions and accessories

Wheelchair repairs

Wheelchair lifts and ramps

• Your local school district's special education office may have additional suggestions.

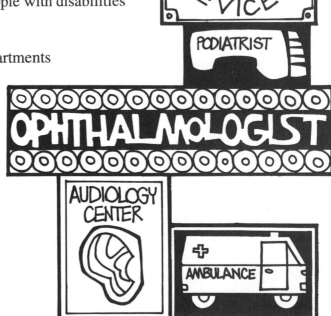

GUEST SPEAKERS

Resource people working with various local community service organizations can be willing volunteers for guest speakers. Many service organizations also support special causes and have access to printed information or videos for classroom presentations. Try contacting some of the following:

- Community college, especially the high-tech center or educational assistance center
- Special education teachers in local school districts
- Parents of children who are disabled
- Lions Club, especially for disabilities of vision or hearing
- Kiwanis Club
- Shriner's, especially for resources regarding crippled children
- Optimist Club
- Special Olympics (see pages 53-54)

When you or a student representative calls, be sure to share the following information. Explain in specific terms what you would like the guest to talk about.

When you call . . .
____ Specify the age, grade level, and number of students in the classroom.
____ Suggest a length for the presentation. (Attention spans vary, so give a minimum and maximum time.)
____ Verify the date and time of the presentation.
____ Explain that a confirmation notice will be sent, including
- directions to the classroom (along with a map)
- details for the office sign-in procedure
- parking location/permit and/or nearest handicapped parking location

After you call . . .
____ Send the confirmation notice, maps, etc., to the speaker.
____ Invite other guests to listen, such as the principal, another class, or someone from a local newspaper.

During the presentation . . .
____ Introduce your guest(s) to the students by name.
____ Set up a podium, table, chair, or whatever is needed for your speaker.
____ Arrange a listening and viewing area for the children.
____ Take photos or videos only with prior permission.
____ Emphasize to the class that there are no right or wrong questions.

After the presentation . . .
____ Send the guest speaker a thank-you note written by a class representative.
____ Do a culminating activity with the class.
- Make a poster with photos from the day or show and discuss a videotape.
- Have students draw pictures and make a scrapbook of the event.

GUEST SPEAKERS

Guest speakers will help your students see that people with disabilities work as doctors, lawyers, and clerks and in other jobs in the community. They can demonstrate that people with disabilities share the same thoughts, feelings, and goals as nondisabled people. For a student who has a disability, a guest speaker who is disabled can be a valuable role model.

Here is a sample letter to send to your guest speaker.

School Letterhead

Date

Dear _____:

Our class is looking forward to your visit with us on _____. If you would like to bring printed information to share, please bring enough for a group of ___. The following are a few questions we wrote down to ask you during your visit:

How did you become disabled? (Please answer children's unspoken concern, Can I catch what you have?)
What special challenges have you faced? How have you dealt with them?
What special tools do you use every day to make life easier for you? (You could talk about the telephone, Braille machines, computers, adaptive devices, transportation vehicles, animal helpers, etc. Please bring any of the devices or objects you use and share them with us.)
What are the things we should or should not do to help you?

A map and other materials are enclosed. We are looking forward to your visit.

Sincerely,

Questions That Pertain to Specific Disabilities
You may also want to include some of the following questions in your letter.

Blind or Visually Impaired
Do you watch TV? What can you eat if you can't see your food? Do you dream in color? Do you enjoy being outside or are you scared you will fall? How do you go to the bathroom?

Hearing Impaired
How do you watch TV? Do you drive a car? Do you go to movies? What happens when you have no paper or pencil to write a message?

In a Wheelchair
How difficult is it to go to the bathroom? What do you do when it rains? Can you drive a car? Do you go to amusement parks?

Remember to keep a scrapbook!

FAMOUS PEOPLE WITH DISABILITIES

Jose Vincente Alvarado	1931-	artist, leprosy, degenerative bone disease
Hans Christian Anderson	1805-1875	author of fairy tales, LD
Tim Baley	1954-	musician, mental challenges
Billy Barty	1924-	actor, person of short stature
Ludwig Van Beethoven	1770-1827	musician, deaf
Harry Belafonte	1927-	singer, actor, producer, human rights activist, LD
George Burns	1896-	actor, comedian, LD
Ray Charles	1930-	musician, composer, singer, blind
Cher	1946-	singer, actress, LD
Young Duk Cho	1975-	artist, hearing impaired
Agatha Christie	1890-1976	British novelist, LD
Winston Churchill	1874-1947	Prime Minster of Great Britain, LD
Max Cleland	1942-	Head of Veterans Administration, amputee
Tom Cruise	1962-	actor, LD
Leonardo da Vinci	1452-1519	artist, scientist, LD
Henri de Toulouse-Lautrec	1864-1901	artist, physically challenged
Joan Didion	1934-	author, multiple sclerosis
Walt Disney	1901-1966	animator, cartoonist, created Disneyland, labeled "slow"
Thomas Edison	1847-1931	inventor, industrialist, LD
Albert Einstein	1879-1955	scientist, LD
Jim Eisenreich	1959-	baseball athlete, Tourette syndrome
Jose Feliciano	1945	singer, guitarist, blind
Terry Fox	1958-1981	runner, amputee with cancer
Annette Funicello	1942-	actress, multiple sclerosis
Whoopi Goldberg	1950-	actress, comedian, LD
Stephen Hawking	1942-	physicist, Cambridge University, Lou Gehrig's disease
Katharine Hepburn	1909-	actress, Parkinson's disease
Homer	8th century BC	Greek poet, blind
Bruce Jenner	1949-	Olympic Decathlon Gold Medalist, LD
Liu Jingshing	1955-	artist, quadriplegic
James Earl Jones	1931-	actor, stutterer from age 6 to 14
Dr. I. King Jordan	1943-	first president of Gallaudet University, deaf
Helen Keller	1880-1968	author, lecturer, deaf and blind
Charles Kranel	1893-1991	filmmaker, deaf
Harold Krents	1947-	attorney, blind

LD — learning differences or disability

FAMOUS PEOPLE WITH DISABILITIES

John "Charlie" Leal	1905–	actor, person of short stature
John Lennon	1940-1980	singer, musician, songwriter with the Beatles, LD
Michael Maranjo	1949–	sculptor, LD
Marlee Matlin	1965–	actress, deaf
John Milton	1608-1674	poet, author, blind
Isaac Newton	1642-1727	scientist, mentally ill
General George Patton	1885-1945	American general/tank commander, LD
Itzhak Perlman	1945–	concert violinist, paralyzed from waist down
Richard Pryor	1940–	actor, comedian, multiple sclerosis
Nelson Rockefeller	1908-1979	politician, U.S. Vice President, LD
Franklin Delano Roosevelt	1882-1945	32nd U.S. President, had polio at age 39, paralyzed
Theodore Roosevelt	1858-1919	26th U.S. President, asthma, partially sighted
Tarah Lynne Schaeffer	1984–	Sesame Street cast member, osteogenesis imperfecta (OI)
George Shearing	1919–	composer, pianist, blind
Tom Sullivan	1947–	actor, singer, blind
Joni Eareckson Tada	1949–	lecturer, artist, author, quadriplegic since age 17
Alec Templeton	1910-1963	pianist, composer, blind
James Thurber	1894-1961	cartoonist, humorist, visually impaired
Harriet Tubman	1821-1913	abolitionist, organizer of underground railroad during Civil War, acquired brain injury
Vincent Van Gogh	1853-1890	artist, mentally ill
Bree Walker	1953–	TV newscaster, syndillism
James E. West	1876-1948	first Chief Executive of Boy Scouts of America, tubercular hip
Heather Whitestone	1973–	1994 Miss America, deaf
Bill Wilson	1896-1971	founder of Alcoholics Anonymous, LD
Woodrow Wilson	1856-1924	27th U.S. President, LD
Stevie Wonder	1950–	musician, blind

LD — learning differences or disability

FOLLOW-UP ACTIVITIES FOR "FAMOUS PEOPLE WITH DISABILITIES"

Activities for Use in the Primary Grades

- Ask students to choose a name from the list and write a brief report about the person's life. Have students find information on the person's specific disability and how the person met the challenges he or she faced.

- Hold a life history week or combine the students' biographical mini-reports with curriculum units or news events.

- Collect photos or pictures of famous people with disabilities. Ask a parent volunteer or aide to compile a poster on each famous person. The volunteer or teaching aide can present the information to the class and lead a weekly discussion on a famous person with a special need.

- Bring in a current newspaper article about a child with a disability to read to the class. Use this article as an opening to a discussion on famous people with disabilities.

- Create a bulletin board of people with disabilities in the news. Post current newspaper articles. Have each child prepare a biographical statement about one newsmaker's strengths and weaknesses.

Activities for Use in the Upper Grades

- Ask students to choose a name from the list and write a report. Students should research the person's life, specific disability, accomplishments, and ways the person has met these challenges.

- Have students sort or graph the list by category: entertainer, artist, musician, philosopher, politician, etc. Ask students to add local heroes to the list.

- Have students share their research reports orally with the class. Then have the class sort the names on the list by specific disability or create a time line showing oldest to youngest, living or dead.

- Have students practice and polish presentations based on their reports. Then form teams to visit classrooms with younger children to present their information.

VOCABULARY: SAY IT WITH MEANING

The words used to talk about disabilities are constantly changing. Often words convey the wrong image of being disabled. Being aware and sensitive is the first step toward correct usage. When you're in doubt, ask individuals with a disability for their preference. The key in talking about any disability is to place the person first so that the person has more importance than the disability.

Say	Instead of
child with a disability	handicapped child
person with cerebral palsy	palsied, C.P., or spastic
person who has . . .	who is afflicted with, suffering from, a victim of
without speech, nonverbal	mute or dumb
developmentally delayed	slow
has an emotional disorder or mental illness	is crazy or insane
deaf or hearing impaired	deaf and dumb
uses a wheelchair	is confined to a wheelchair
person with retardation	retarded person
person with epilepsy	epileptic
person with Down syndrome	mongoloid
has a learning disability	is learning disabled
nondisabled	normal, healthy
has a physical disability	is crippled
congenital disability	birth defect
condition	disease (unless the disability is a disease)
has a seizure disorder	has fits
cleft pallet	harelip
mobility impaired	lame
medically involved or chronically ill	sickly
person who is paralyzed	invalid or paralytic
person of short stature	dwarf or midget

A DRAWING CHALLENGE

It's difficult to imagine that a child who doesn't need glasses and who seems as smart as anyone else could have difficulty reading, writing, or just copying letters. After all, the letters in the English alphabet are the *simplest* combinations of lines and curves. So is this drawing. Take a good look at it and then follow the directions below.

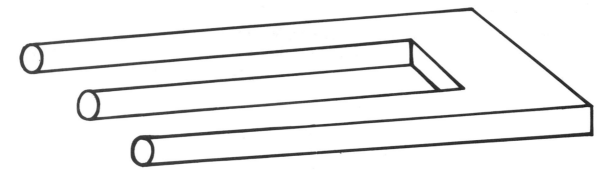

What You Do

1. Study the shape for thirty seconds. Then turn the page over and, on another piece of paper, take thirty seconds to draw the shape from memory.

2. Did you have trouble? Then, on a second piece of paper, take thirty seconds to copy the shape while you look at it. Not so easy either, is it?

Trying to understand and draw this shape isn't exactly the same as having a learning problem. But this exercise shows you what some children face every day. It helps you understand why they have difficulty learning seemingly simple things like reading and writing.

DISABILITY SAFETY CHECKLIST

What You Do

Divide into teams and check various home, school, and shopping environments such as the grocery store, drug store, or discount store for disabled accessibility and safety hazards. Make a chart like the one below for each location you evaluate. Check whether items or locations are safe or unsafe. Record any hazards you observe.

Potential Hazards for People with Disabilities

safe	unsafe	hazard	(areas to evaluate; record any hazards observed)
❏	❏	❏	sidewalks (cracks or uneven)
❏	❏	❏	walkways (steep, hilly, or sloping)
❏	❏	❏	steps (uneven or too small)
❏	❏	❏	overhead hazards (low branches, wires, or ropes and/or low-hanging flowerpots, mobiles, or light fixtures)
❏	❏	❏	clutter or debris (on walkways or pathways, at entrances)
❏	❏	❏	doors with unmarked semi-circle openings
❏	❏	❏	doors too heavy to push open without help
❏	❏	❏	door handles too high or too low
❏	❏	❏	sharp corners on furniture
❏	❏	❏	fire extinguishers (missing or inaccessible)
❏	❏	❏	telephone (too high or hard to get to)
❏	❏	❏	television (hard to reach controls)
❏	❏	❏	counter space (too high to be used)
❏	❏	❏	other items out of reach
❏	❏	❏	cupboard doors (left open or difficult to open or reach)
❏	❏	❏	furniture (rolls too easily and has no safety locks, has sharp corners, obstructs traffic)
❏	❏	❏	other safety hazards (describe)

Follow-Up Activities

- **Poster Making:** Have team members draw pictures of any safety hazards you listed in your charts.

- **Photo Opportunities:** Photograph safe situations at home or at school. Create a poster, album, or display of your photos to share with the class. If your team has no camera available, check with your teacher to see if the school can provide a disposable camera you can use.

ACCESSIBILITY SURVEY: PREPARATION AND FOLLOW-UP

Show students the handicap or wheelchair-accessible symbol. Ask students to give their views on what the sign means. Be sure to make the point that this sign identifies buildings or locations that have special facilities for people in wheelchairs or for those with physical disabilities.

- Make sure students understand that accessible means easy to approach or enter.
- Provide tape measures and send students out to measure various sites and facilities at school.

Follow-Up Activities
- Prepare an Accessibility Kit or packet for each child in the class. Have each student take the kit home and make an accessibility survey. In each kit, include a checklist, a tape measure, and a note to parents that explains the details of the project.
- Have students use their Accessibility Kits to measure facilities at local businesses, stores, or shopping areas. You might make this activity a field trip or assign it to pairs or teams of students as homework.

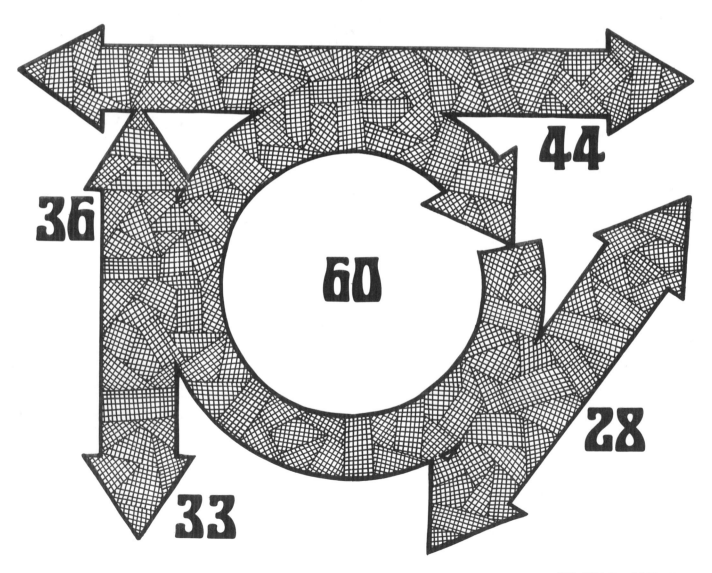

Survey: How Accessible Is This Place?

Accessibility is important for all people. People who use walkers or wheelchairs want to shop, use the library, and cross streets by themselves. Adequate space for wheelchairs and walkers is important.

Wheelchairs and walkers are usually thirty-three inches wide, but most doorways are only thirty inches wide. A normal parking space is about five feet wide, but buses or vans with wheelchair lifts need seven to eight feet. Airplane aisles and bathrooms are often so small that people in wheelchairs can't use them.

What You Need
- With your team or partner, get an Accessibility Kit from your teacher.

What You Do
- Using the kit, measure each item listed below and record the measurement on the chart. If the actual measurement is less than what is required for handicap access, subtract the actual measurement from the "inches required" and record the amount in the column marked "difference."

Survey of Facilities for Handicap Accessibility

Item	Inches required	Actual Inches	Difference
walkways	44 inches wide		
halls, corridors	44 inches wide		
aisles	44 inches wide		
rest room stalls	60 inches turning space		
doorknobs	36 inches high		
doorways	36 inches wide		
towel dispensers	40 inches high		
water fountains	33 inches high		
light switches	48 inches high		
phones	54 inches high (hand set)		
sinks	29–34 inches high		
fire alarms	48 inches high		

WHEELCHAIR GUIDELINES

Meeting an individual who is in a wheelchair can be uncomfortable for some people who are unsure how to act. Parents or adults with small children are often faced with an awkward or even embarrassing moment when their curious child asks about the individual in the chair. A child's natural curiosity needs to be satisfied so that he or she does not become fearful or misinformed. Most wheelchair users are not offended by questions that people ask them about their disability or their chair. The guidelines below address general points of information that may not apply in all instances.

1. **Avoid assuming that wheelchair users are sick or paralyzed.**
    Although wheelchairs are often associated with hospitals, they are used for a variety of noncontagious disabilities. Don't classify all persons in wheelchairs as sick.

2. **Act natural.**
    Using expressions like "running along" when talking with a person in a wheelchair is a common occurrence. It's likely that the wheelchair user expresses the same thoughts. Don't make the situation awkward by speaking unnaturally.

3. **Ask permission.**
    Ask the wheelchair user if he or she would like assistance before you help. It may be necessary for the person to give you some instructions. An unexpected push could throw the wheelchair user off balance.

4. **Be respectful.**
    A person's wheelchair is part of his or her personal body space and should be treated with respect. Don't hang or lean on the chair unless you have the person's permission.

5. **Speak directly to a person in a wheelchair.**
    Speak directly to the person in the chair, and if the conversation is lengthy, sit down or kneel to get on the same level as the wheelchair user. Don't exclude wheelchair users from conversations. They may not have the mobility you do, but they usually have excellent hearing. Also, avoid the degrading gesture of patting a person in a wheelchair on the head.

6. **Don't think or speak of wheelchair users as being confined to their chairs.**
    Be aware that persons who use wheelchairs are not confined to them. When a person transfers out of the wheelchair to a chair, toilet, or car, do not move the wheelchair out of reach. Ask where the person prefers that the chair be placed.

7. **Be aware that some wheelchair users can walk.**
    Each individual chair user has different mobility capabilities. Some users can walk with aids such as walkers, canes, braces, or crutches. Some individuals use wheelchairs to conserve energy and to move about more quickly.

Activities

*   Borrow a wheelchair and spend a morning or afternoon roaming around a shopping mall to simulate the everyday experiences that a wheelchair user faces. Make a list of your impressions to share with your class.

*   With an older group, set up a hidden video camera to tape students' honest reactions to meeting a person in a wheelchair.

Parking Spaces for People With Disabilities

How large are parking spaces at the grocery store or at the mall? Are vans or buses that have lifts for people in wheelchairs able to park up close to the store's entrance? Is there enough space to allow the wheelchair apparatus to descend safely?

A normal car needs a parking space of about five feet. A person with a disability may need additional room to maneuver around and get into a wheelchair. A bus or van with a lift needs an area about eight feet wide.

What You Do

1. **Survey the parking lots of local businesses.** Go to local business or shopping areas and do the following:

   - Count the number of spaces designated as handicapped parking. _____

   - Measure the width of a regular parking space and a handicapped space.
     Regular space _____ Handicapped space _____

   - Observe and count how many handicapped spaces are filled by cars displaying the legal placard. _____

   - Observe and count how many handicapped spaces are filled by cars not displaying the legal placard. _____

   - Observe an individual with a disability using a parking space. Describe in writing how easy or difficult the space is to use.

   - List any recommendations or suggestions you have for this parking lot.

2. **Voice your thoughts!** Have a classroom discussion about what you found. Then, write a letter complimenting the business for providing this valuable assistance for people with disabilities; or in a letter to your local legislator, owner of the business property, or appropriate government official, describe any problems you observed and share your concerns.

3. **Check license plates for symbols.** Some states place the letters DP on the license plate to denote "disabled person." This action has advantages and disadvantages. What ones can you think of? On a separate piece of paper, list some advantages and disadvantages.

   Other states put the access symbol on the plate. What does your state do? What is good or bad about your state's policy? Report your conclusions and/or concerns in an opinion essay or letter and submit it to the school newspaper.

CREATE YOUR OWN PARKING REMINDER

Find out how many tickets or reminders are written in your area each week because individuals have parked illegally in designated handicapped parking spots. Who gives the tickets? Are reminder cards used? What is the fine? Are these individuals asked to do community service with the disabled instead of paying the fine? In some communities, disabled people are hired as meter personnel. Is this the case in your community?

What You Can Do

1. Get answers to the questions above. Then use what you found out to make a list of suggestions you can give to your local law enforcement agency.

2. In the illustrated space below, create your own reminder card to place on vehicles that are parked illegally in handicapped parking spots.

3. As a class project, monitor the school parking lot for a couple of hours a day and put students' reminder cards on illegally parked vehicles.

4. If your school parking lot does not have a designated handicapped parking spot, obtain permission from the principal and school district to paint one. Make this a class project.

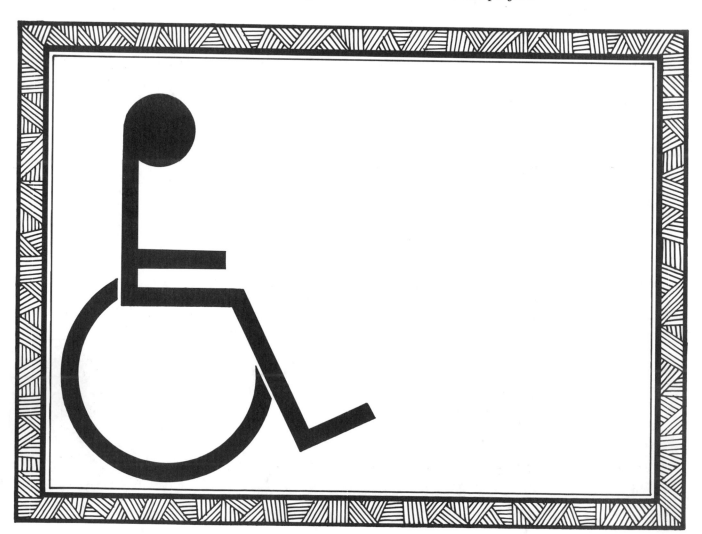

MOBILITY OR IMMOBILITY?

Purpose: To help children understand the frustration of not having full mobility or the use of all body parts

What You Need

To make one restraint device, you will need the following materials:
- cloth webbing or heavy-duty tape
- tape measure
- scissors
- sewing machine or needles and heavy thread

What You Do

1. Cut one strip of webbing 42" long and $1\frac{1}{4}$" wide.

2. Cut another strip 9" long and $1\frac{1}{4}$" wide. (Cut longer strips for adults.)

3. Fold back $5\frac{1}{2}$" at each end of the long strip. Stitch down a $1\frac{1}{2}$" section, joining each end to the strip and making two 8" loops.

4. Stitch the short strip to the long strip at the point where one of the loops has been stitched down.

5. Fold up $3\frac{1}{2}$" of the short strip and stitch it down to make one 6" loop.

6. To put on the restraint, have the child lay the long strip over his or her right shoulder and pull one end under the left arm. Slide the free end of the long strip through the loop on the short strip. Tell the child to put his or her hands in the 8" loops at either end of the long strip.

7. Have the child perform daily activities while wearing the restraint. With hands restrained close to the child's chest, have the child do math, write, tie his or her shoes, or eat lunch.

Observe restrained children closely to be sure the frustration level stays within manageable limits for each individual child.

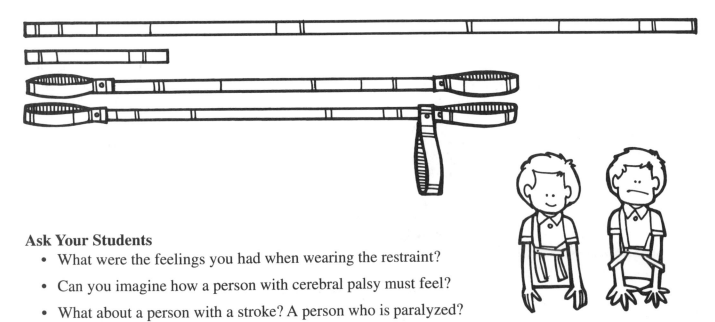

Ask Your Students

- What were the feelings you had when wearing the restraint?

- Can you imagine how a person with cerebral palsy must feel?

- What about a person with a stroke? A person who is paralyzed?

OBSTACLE COURSE EVENT

Make arrangements with the school administration to cordon off a section of the school playground and set up an obstacle course that simulates what it is like to be disabled. Set up various centers within the area. Allow enough time for students to complete each activity without hurrying. The last activity should be a debriefing center where a student facilitator under the supervision of an adult asks participants, "What were your feelings?" The facilitator should lead a brief discussion based on comments from students.

Choose from the ideas listed below or others included in this book, or use your own ideas to design your activity centers. Prepare materials and instruction sheets or posters for each center you create.

Suggestions for Activity Centers

1. *Writing:* The student writes his or her name and phone number with the nondominant hand, the one not normally used for writing.

2. *Coordination:* The student walks in a sack around a short, obstacle-filled path. Have an able-bodied student spotter present to ensure safety.

3. *Coordination:* The student walks with his or her thighs taped together.

4. *Mobility:* With feet tied together, the student crawls through a series of obstacles without using his or her legs.

5. *Small motor control:* Using the last two fingers of his or her nondominant hand, the student picks up a pencil and places it in a small box.

6. *Upper chest mobility:* With one arm tied to the student's chest, he or she tries to bounce a ball or hit a tether ball. (Use the directions on page 51 to make mobility straps.)

7. *Vision:* Wearing wax paper glasses, the student tries to put together a jigsaw puzzle.

8. *Vision:* Wearing a winter cap over his or her eyes, the student tries to color a page from a coloring book.

9. *Reading:* The student tries to read a simple page by looking only at its reflection in a mirror.

10. *Mobility:* Sitting in a wheelchair, the student tries to navigate a simple course where objects are placed too close together.

11. *Disabled guest speaker:* Have a person who is visually impaired bring his or her guide dog and demonstrate how the dog performs. Or, have a student who is disabled be the speaker and tell how he or she became disabled. Prepare one or two questions for young students to ask the guest. Ask older students to create their own questions.

12. *Debriefing:* An experienced student or facilitator asks each student, "What were your feelings?" or "How did it feel?" Videotape students' reactions to replay later.

Culminating Activity

• Have students design and supervise an obstacle course to introduce another class to disability awareness. Planning and executing this project will pull together all of the new information and insights students have gained during their study of the challenges faced by people with special needs.

SPECIAL OLYMPICS

The Special Olympics was created in 1968 by Eunice Kennedy Shriver. The event is modeled after the Olympic Games. The competitors are youngsters and adults with disabilities.

Special Olympic events provide an opportunity for the disabled to train and compete in such sports as basketball, bowling, canoeing, cycling, floor hockey, gymnastics, horseback riding, ice skating, power lifting, roller-skating, skiing, soccer, softball, swimming, table tennis, team handball, tennis, track and field, and volleyball. Participants compete in different divisions, depending on their age and ability.

Competitors train in programs offered through schools or local communities. In the United States, games are held at local, area, and state levels every year. The scores and records from competitions at the state level are evaluated, and a number of individuals are chosen to take part at the national level. This selection is based on merit, not ability. Coaches and committees make the decision based on a variety of factors.

For international competition, a lottery system is used to draw competitors from the pool of national gold and silver medal winners. Over 100 countries participate worldwide, holding games every year or every other year. The International Special Olympic Games consist of both summer and winter games that occur by turns every two years.

Competitors never pay to compete in the Special Olympics, and the program receives no assistance from the federal government. Instead, each local chapter holds fund-raisers for the year-round program of training and events.

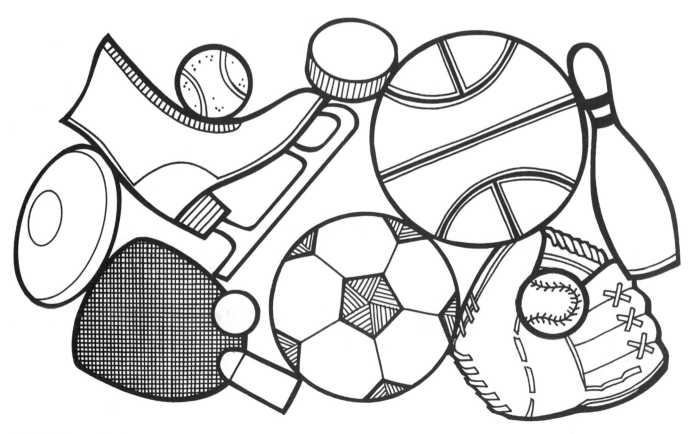

SPECIAL OLYMPICS

Do you know anyone who has competed in the Special Olympics or who helps the organization? If you do, ask this person to tell you more about what it was like to compete or what he or she does to help. Then share what you learn with your classmates.

Local Special Olympics chapters can often use volunteers to help with events or with fund-raising. Here's how to find out about getting involved.

What You Can Do

- To get more information or to learn more about volunteering, call the national organization in Washington, DC, (202) 628-3630, and ask for the phone number of the chapter nearest you.

- Watch for newspaper articles about kids in your community competing in the Special Olympics. Invite a participant to visit your class and tell you what it's like to compete.

- Make a bulletin board display on the Special Olympics. Include newspaper articles, letters from competitors or local volunteers, pictures of events, etc.

- Have a Special Olympics at your school. Use ideas from your study of disabilities to design competitions for the event. Participate in these competitions using various restraints and other devices that limit your mobility. Share your feelings with classmates on what it felt like to compete in the event.

ASSISTIVE TECHNOLOGY

The following list contains common software programs and hardware devices used by students with disabilities.

Alternative Keyboards: options that include software images of a regular keyboard, chording keyboards, programmable keyboards, and/or miniature keyboards.

Keyguards: hard plastic covers with a hole for each key.

Switches: devices that allow the operator to use a different part of his or her body to control input to a computer. Switches come in a variety of sizes, shapes, and colors. The correct choices are usually highlighted on the monitor.

Touch Screens: software built into the computer or a device placed on the computer monitor that allows a person to touch the screen to select an answer.

Arm and Wrist Supports: devices that stabilize and support the arms and wrists of the user during typing.

Joysticks and Trackballs: devices that can be plugged into the computer's mouse port to control the cursor on the screen.

Voice Recognition: software and hardware that allows a person to input data by voice rather than keyboard.

ASSISTIVE TECHNOLOGY

Scanner: a device that converts the printed page into a computer file. Optical character recognition (OCR) software works with the scanner.

Grammar and Spell Checkers: software programs that display errors in a document as well as suggestions for correction.

Braille: software that allows a user to operate a keyboard as a Brailler or to translate print characters into Braille.

Refreshable Braille Displays: a device that provides tactile output of information highlighted by the cursor. The Braille characters change instantly as the cursor moves.

Speech Synthesizers: a device that speaks to the user and is used in combination with software.

Screen Enlargement: software that enlarges characters or symbols on the monitor.

Learning Skill Programs: software programs that focus on improving skills in reading, writing, math, etc.

Word Prediction Programs: software programs that allow the user to select a desired word from an on-screen list. The user need only choose the number/letter preceding or associated with a word and the word is instantly inserted into the text.

COMPUTERS: THE GREAT EQUALIZERS

Many children with disabilities enjoy using computers. People with disabilities are discovering the joys of communicating with technology. Databases and bulletin board networks are springing up to serve computer users with special needs.

What You Do

Write the letter for each human ability next to the assistive computer hardware or software that best supports that ability. *Letters may match more than one computer option.*

When people are unable to . . .

A. type with steady fingers
B. talk
C. speak clearly
D. move their arms
E. move their bodies
F. see well or at all
G. see clearly
H. spell
I. write
J. compute
K. hear
L. use both hands

Computers can provide . . .

1. ___ word prediction programs
2. ___ touch screens
3. ___ speech synthesizers
4. ___ scanners (optical character recognition)
5. ___ screen enlargement
6. ___ voice recognition
7. ___ joysticks and trackballs
8. ___ key guards
9. ___ Braille programs
10. ___ switches
11. ___ spell checkers
12. ___ alternative keyboards
13. ___ wrist and arm supports

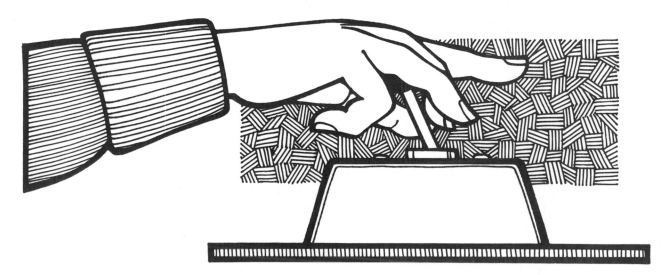

• This page is adapted from *Spinal Network* (1987), S. Maddox (ed.). Boulder, CO: Spinal Network and Sam Maddox. Reprinted with permission.

COMMUNITY AWARENESS DAY

The purpose of Community Awareness Day is to make people in the community aware of the problems people with disabilities encounter every minute and hour of their lives. There are many ways to conduct a community awareness day. Your class may decide to sponsor an awareness day just for the local school or in conjunction with another community event such as a health expo. Your awareness day can follow these formats: workshop or seminar sessions, simulated daily living activities, or a community-wide awareness day with varied activities.

After a few hours of participation in an awareness day, a whole new thought process opens for most people. The few hours spent simulating life as a person in a wheelchair, on crutches, with a dominant arm restrained, with ears plugged, or with eyes blindfolded creates a lasting impression.

"What if I really were disabled? How much would my world change? How would it affect my job?" These are some of the questions asked during and after an awareness day experience. Participants will acquire a new appreciation of the inaccessibility and accessibility of streets, sidewalks, and buildings in the participating community.

Organizational Tasks
____ Find sponsors or funding sources.
____ Arrange publicity: news releases, posters, signs, photos, radio announcements, etc.
____ Secure sufficient equipment to simulate disabilities: wheelchairs, blindfolds, slings and safety pins to tie dominant arms, ear plugs or cotton to simulate hearing loss, crutches, and mobility straps.
____ Schedule speakers for workshop presentations.
____ Arrange for a site: parking lot, hall, or meeting rooms for presentations.
____ Send invitations and/or announcements.
____ Arrange for transportation vehicles and drivers: vans with lifts, a local wheelchair service, and private cars.
____ Obtain a registration table and name tags.

Ways to Find Participants
• Contact local organizations of citizens with disabilities and people who work with them. Invite members to be workshop presenters, registration assistants, etc.

• Try to pair a person with a disability (who will act as a resource person during the entire event) with an able-bodied individual.

• Arrange to have demonstrations of Braille transcription by hand or computer.

• Invite people from pet therapy groups to put on demonstrations.

KEEPING A SCRAPBOOK

With each guest speaker, field trip, or awareness activity your class completes, add another page or two to a class scrapbook. This activity does two things:

- It reinforces visually what took place during the visit.

- When scrapbooks are looked at again, individual children or the class as a whole can recall the experience and build upon the ideas presented or discovered.

Scrapbook Suggestions
- Put a parent volunteer in charge of keeping the scrapbook up to date.

- Have an upper-grade classroom send in a video production team to film each event.

- Contact a local bank or active community organization for a donation to help with expenses for a camera, film, and photo developing.

- Contact a representative from a major camera company to find out if the company's educational program foundation can help by providing free cameras and learning materials for your classroom.

- Use the scrapbook and any videotapes as visual learning tools for an open house or back-to-school night. All parents enjoy seeing their children in photographs or on film.

BULLETIN BOARD AND POSTER IDEAS

We All Come in Different Packages

Cover empty boxes with butcher, shelf, adhesive-backed, or wrapping paper in assorted bright colors. Use marking pens or paint to add facial features and other details. Decorate the boxes with buttons, fabric scraps, felt, paper, and ribbon to represent children with special needs. Add eyeglasses, hats, suspenders, and ties for a realistic touch. Stack the boxes against a wall or use push pins to attach them to the bulletin board.

Candy Jar

Draw a large jar filled with jelly beans or the class's favorite candy. Color in one piece of candy for every positive observation that a student makes concerning disability awareness. Bringing in a newspaper clipping, telling about a job that a person with a disability is performing locally, or sharing an observation about an activity with a classmate with a disability would all qualify for coloring in a piece of candy. Keep a count of how many pieces are colored in each week. This activity helps students recall past discoveries and keeps the interest in awareness activities high. When the entire jar is colored in, have a real jelly bean party! Add the caption "Sweet Discoveries!" (If you have students with diabetes in your class, substitute sugarless candy.)

In the News

Check with your local newspaper about past or future stories featuring members of the community who are disabled. Ask students to bring in any stories and photos they find and to post them on a special bulletin board. Use the caption "Newsworthy People!"

Guest Speakers

Take photos, with the permission of guest speakers, and prominently display them along with a brief write-up of the class discussion. Write captions that include the names of the guest speakers.

Factual Information

Call one of the 800 telephone numbers listed on pages 185 to 187 and inquire about information and posters for the classroom. Use any materials received in a bulletin board display.

CHAPTER 3
THE BRAIN–A COMPUTER IN CHARGE OF LEARNING

INTRODUCTION

In the decade from 1976 to 1986, scientists and researchers learned more about how the mind functions than in all previous years of human existence. From that decade, some general theories of intelligence emerged: theories of mediated learning experience, theories of multiple kinds of intelligence, and techniques to enhance thinking on both sides of the brain — the left for serial thinking and the right for holistic thinking. Brain research has indicated to parents and educators that schools need to shift to different teaching methods to "catch the way kids learn."

Such a shift in teaching methods would greatly benefit children with learning disabilities. These children exhibit a wide range of symptoms, including problems with reading, mathematics, comprehension, writing, spoken language, and reasoning abilities. Hyperactivity, inattention, and perceptual coordination may also be associated with learning disabilities but are not learning disabilities themselves. The primary characteristic of a learning disability is a significant difference between a child's achievement in some areas and his or her overall intelligence.

This section introduces:

- myths and facts about disabilities

- the brain: what it does and how to protect this valuable center of thinking and doing

- ways people are unique: similarities and differences, talents and feelings

- activities that simulate different styles of learning

BRAIN PUZZLE: GETTING YOUR HEAD TOGETHER

Each part of your brain helps your body do something. Sometimes, when people are very sick or when they have been in an accident that caused a head injury, parts of their brain do not function smoothly. They may have trouble doing an activity that's controlled by the injured area of the brain.

What You Do
- Color this picture of "the brain" and glue it onto a thicker piece of paper.
- Cut the puzzle pieces apart on the dotted lines.
- Reassemble the pieces to form "the brain."

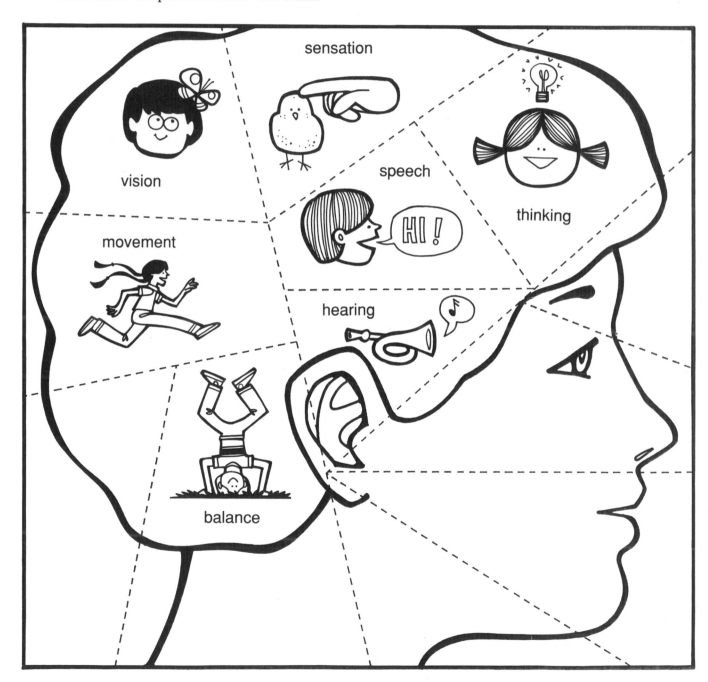

HELMETS AND PROTECTIVE GEAR

The main function of a helmet is to reduce the harm caused by a blow to the head when playing certain sports or games or riding two-wheel vehicles. Each state has its own laws governing the use of protective helmets when riding bicycles and motorcycles. There are also headgear regulations for a variety of sports and activities.

Things to Remember
1. Wear a helmet or protective head gear in the correct way (with the chin strap on).

2. Good fit is important. The helmet should fit snugly, but not uncomfortably. Do not wear a helmet that is too large or too small.

Check any activities that require wearing protective head gear.

❏ sewing	❏ ATV riding
❏ mountain climbing	❏ snowmobile riding
❏ walking	❏ playing pogs or marbles
❏ ice skating	❏ midget car racing
❏ bike riding	❏ speed car racing
❏ in-line skating	❏ fishing
❏ skate boarding	❏ ballet
❏ tobogganing	❏ rowing
❏ wrestling	❏ sailing
❏ hockey	❏ working a puzzle
❏ street hockey	❏ doing dishes
❏ reading	❏ surf boarding
❏ motorcycle riding	❏ doing math problems
❏ moped riding	❏ watching a video

Remember: No helmet can protect you from all possible injuries, but it may mean the difference between a minor injury and serious head trauma that changes the rest of your life. It pays to be safe.

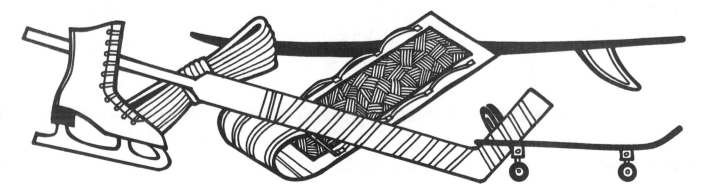

ALL PEOPLE HAVE FEELINGS

People come in different packages, or bodies. They look different from one another. Some are tall and some are short. Some have a sturdy build, while others are thin. People have different abilities. Some are strong and well coordinated, while others find physical tasks difficult. Some are able to sing well, throw a ball accurately, or work math problems quickly. Others have trouble doing all of these things.

All people have feelings. They are sensitive about how they look and about what they can do. They may feel bad if they look different from other people or if they can't do what others are able to do. They may be hurt when other people point out their inability or make fun of their appearance. What are you sensitive about?

What You Do

Check the boxes beside the things you don't want people to make fun of or tease you about.

❑ my artificial limb
❑ my athletic ability
❑ my blindness
❑ my bowed legs
❑ my braces
❑ my burn scars
❑ my cane
❑ my clothes
❑ my complexion
❑ my coordination
❑ my crooked spine
❑ my crossed eyes
❑ my crutches
❑ my deafness
❑ my dimples
❑ my ears
❑ my feet
❑ my fingernails
❑ my freckles

❑ my glasses
❑ my grades
❑ my hair
❑ my hands
❑ my hearing aid
❑ my height
❑ my knock-knees
❑ my laugh
❑ my moles
❑ my musical ability
❑ my nearsighted vision
❑ my nose
❑ my scar
❑ my shape
❑ my speech
❑ my teeth
❑ my toes
❑ my voice
❑ my warts

ALL PEOPLE HAVE TALENTS AND DISABILITIES

Nobody can do everything well. Activities that are easy for some people are difficult or even impossible for others. Indicate how well you can do each of the things listed below by putting an X in one of the boxes.

	For Me It's			I've Never Tried It
	Easy	Hard	Impossible	
answering a question in class				
climbing a tree				
cutting with scissors				
doing long division				
doing magic tricks				
drawing a picture				
finding something out				
growing a plant				
ice skating				
jumping on a pogo stick				
jumping rope				
knitting				
making cookies				
memorizing a part in a play				
playing a musical instrument				
playing chess				
playing marbles or pogs				
playing soccer				
programming a VCR				
riding a bicycle				
riding a horse				
roller skating				
running fast				
skipping				
stamp collecting				
swimming				
taking a test				
throwing a ball				
training a dog				
tying a bow				
using a computer				
using a hammer				
using a sewing machine				
walking on stilts				
whistling				
whittling				
writing a story				

DISABILITY MYTH GAME

This game can be played by small groups or the entire class.

What You Do

- To prepare the myth cards, duplicate pages 66–68. Cut along the solid lines and fold along the broken lines so the words are on the outside. Then staple each card shut.

- To play the game, deal an equal number of cards to each player. Direct players to read both sides of their cards, decide which side is fact, and then lay their cards down in front of them with the facts facing up. Discuss the facts and myths. In this game, as in life, the winners are those who can tell fact from myth.

1a You can't always tell if people have a disability just by looking at them. 	**1b** You can always tell if people have a disability just by looking at them. 	**2a** A child with a hearing aid hears everything the same as a child without a hearing impairment. 	**2b** A child with a hearing aid does not hear everything the same as a child without a hearing impairment. 
3a A child with a severe hearing loss can learn to speak. 	**3b** A child with a severe hearing loss cannot learn to speak. 	**4a** People who are vision impaired can get around by themselves. 	**4b** People with a vision impairment cannot get around by themselves.
5a People with developmental disabilities don't know or care when others make fun of them. 	**5b** People with developmental disabilities have feelings and can be hurt like everyone else. 	**6a** Not all people with hearing impairments can read lips. 	**6b** All people with hearing impairments can read lips.

DISABILITY MYTH GAME

7a
People with cerebral palsy are developmentally impaired.

7b
People with cerebral palsy may be very intelligent.

8a
Many children with mental impairments look just like other children.

8b
All children with mental impairments look different from other children.

9a
People who are legally blind have no useful vision.

9b
People who are legally blind may be able to see many things.

10a
Every disability has only one cause.

10b
Many disabilities have more than one cause.

11a
Cerebral palsy is a condition, not a contagious disease.

11b
Cerebral palsy is a contagious disease.

12a
Young children and teenagers do get cancer and the HIV virus.

12b
Only adults have cancer and get the HIV virus.

13a
Not all people with a disability are developmentally delayed.

13b
All people with a disability are developmentally delayed.

14a
Children with Down syndrome are always happy and easygoing.

14b
Children with Down syndrome are sometimes sad and angry.

15a
Some forms of diabetes can be controlled with insulin, diet, and exercise.

15b
People with diabetes can never eat sugar.

16a
It is okay to pet or play with a guide dog when it is working.

16b
You should not pet or play with a guide dog when it is working.

17a
Children with disabilities always misbehave.

17b
Like other children, children with disabilities sometimes misbehave.

18a
Closed captions make it possible for the hearing impaired to enjoy videos and TV programs.

18b
Closed captions are a nuisance and make it hard for people with normal hearing to enjoy television.

DISABILITY MYTH GAME

19a With concentration and practice, children with visual impairments can learn to rely on their other senses.	**19b** Children with visual impairments automatically develop their other senses.	**20a** Children with learning differences experience trouble only in reading. 	**20b** Children with learning differences can experience difficulty with reading or math. 
21a Most children with learning disabilities could do better if they worked harder.	**21b** Many children with learning disabilities are working as hard as they can.	**22a** People with vision impairments find it easy to eat food that is served in large pieces and portions.	**22b** People with vision impairments find it easier to eat foods that are served in small pieces.
23a All children with cystic fibrosis are restricted to quiet activities.	**23b** Exercise is beneficial to children with cystic fibrosis.	**24a** Children with learning disabilities don't want friends and don't like to play. 	**24b** Children with learning disabilities want to have friends and like to play.
25a Children with learning disabilities can learn to read.	**25b** Children with learning disabilities cannot learn to read. 	**26a** Children with speech problems may be smart.	**26b** Children with speech problems are not intelligent.
27a People with epilepsy are sick with a contagious disease.	**27b** People with epilepsy do not have a contagious disease.	**28a** Using your eyes does not weaken your vision.	**28b** If people with visual impairments use their eyes too much, their sight will get worse. 
29a The best way to communicate with a person with a hearing impairment is to repeat yourself in a loud voice until the person understands. **HEY!!**	**29b** The best way to communicate with a person with a hearing impairment is to write your message.	**30a** Computers cannot be used by children with disabilities.	**30b** Many adaptive devices help children with disabilities use computers. 

TALKING SOCK PUPPETS

Purpose: To enable children or adults to experience many kinds of disabilities firsthand

What You Need

The materials listed below are for one child to make one puppet. If many children are involved, you will need to increase the quantities and measurements accordingly. If you do not have enough of the disability devices (such as blindfolds, gloves, and eyeglasses) for each child, do this activity with small groups and have children take turns.

- old eyeglasses
- clear nail polish
- cotton swabs
- handkerchief or scarf to use as a blindfold
- sock
- pantyhose for stuffing
- glove
- rubber band
- three-inch tagboard circle
- tacky glue
- felt scraps for facial features
- yarn for hair
- scissors

What You Do

- Prepare glasses by painting the lenses with clear nail polish. Use cotton swabs to put "squiggles" in the polish before it dries.

- Announce to the class that the creative project for the day is making a puppet. This puppet will be made using some special kinds of directions. Each part of the puppet-making activity will simulate a different disability.

- Read the instructions on page 70 to the students out loud. Each instruction in bold italic type simulates a different disability. Make sure every child has followed the simulation instruction before you explain the next step in making the sock puppet.

TALKING SOCK PUPPETS

Put a blindfold over your eyes. *(blindness)*
1. Turn the sock wrong side out.
2. Stuff the sock with pantyhose, from the toe halfway to the heel.

Take off the blindfold and put on the glove. *(poor fine-motor control)*
3. Put the rubber band around the sock to hold the stuffing in. Twist the rubber band several times to make it really tight.

Now take off the glove and watch me. *(deafness)*
(Mouth the directions for steps 4 and 5 so that the children have to lip-read.)
4. Crease the tagboard circle in the middle.
5. Put glue all over one side of the circle. This circle will be the puppet's mouth.

Put on a pair of squiggly glasses. *(vision impairment)*
6. Put the tagboard mouth over the widest part of the sock heel. Hold it for about five minutes, until the glue dries.
7. Turn the sock right side out.

Take off the glasses and put one hand in your pocket or under the table. *(physical disability or lack of small-motor coordination)*
8. Using one hand, cut eyes, nose, and lips from felt.
9. Cut hair from yarn scraps.

Take your hand out of your pocket and finish assembling your puppet.
11. Glue the facial features and the hair to the puppet.
12. Let the glue dry.

Follow-Up Activities
- After the activity, get the children to talk about constructing the puppet. Ask questions: How difficult was it? Why? Which "disability" created the most problems for you?

- Discuss with the children how their temporary disabilities made them feel. Did they feel awkward, frustrated, or angry when tasks that are usually simple became so difficult?

- Have students use their finished puppets to express feelings, to put on a puppet show, or to role play some situations involving people with disabilities.

- Have students use the puppets to act out the poem on pages 198-199.

LEFT AND RIGHT

Scientists have discovered a great deal about how the brain works. The brain is divided into two hemispheres, or halves. They work both together and separately.

The left brain is logical and sequential. The right brain is creative and visual. Each person's brain is unique. Usually a person favors one side of the brain over the other, but some people use both sides equally and are called laterally balanced.

Look at each of the characteristics below. Discuss them with your teacher and class. As a group, decide whether each item is a left- or right-brain characteristic. On the lines below, write each characteristic in the category where you have decided it belongs.

- thinks and sees parts of the idea or task
- rarely feels sad or down in the dumps
- enjoys the melody in musical pieces
- usually enjoys art and creative activities
- thinks in very logical ways
- feels tense about getting things right
- buys things on impulse
- rarely counts change or checks a bill
- enjoys a steady beat when listening to music
- learns quickly from books and lectures
- enjoys math
- has a relaxed attitude that lets things flow

- buys possessions based on value and use
- is usually aware if change is correct
- thinks from whole to part, or holistically
- is very scattered in conversations
- enjoys crossword puzzles
- focuses on facts and figures
- enjoys the sensory feel of fabrics and textures
- enjoys feeling and handling objects
- likes to finish one thing before starting the next
- often experiences hunches
- enjoys watching TV
- remembers faces

Left Brain

_____
_____
_____
_____
_____
_____
_____
_____
_____
_____
_____

Right Brain

_____
_____
_____
_____
_____
_____
_____
_____
_____
_____
_____

- Which set of characteristics is most like you, right-brain or left-brain?

WHICH SIDE DO YOU USE?

Here is a survey to determine which side of your brain controls most of your activities. Remember that the left side of your brain controls the right side of your body, and the right side controls the left side of your body.

What You Do

Read each of the following statements. Quickly, without thinking, make the motion it describes. Then, based on your motion, check the correct answer to each question.

Question	Left	Right
1. Pretend you are kicking a ball. Which foot do you use?	___	___
2. Cross your legs. Which leg is on top?	___	___
3. Fold your arms. Which arm is on top?	___	___
4. Clasp your hands together. Which thumb is on top?	___	___
5. Hold up a paper towel tube and look through it with one eye. Which eye do you use?	___	___
6. Pretend you are reaching for an object. Which hand do you extend?	___	___
7. Look at your answers. Which side of your brain is busiest?	___	___

Kids With Special Needs
©1996–The Learning Works

BRAIN TRAUMA

Accidents that damage the brain are growing more common as children experience the thrills of fast-paced sports activities such as in-line skating and riding motorcycles. The most frequent causes of Traumatic Brain Injury (TBI) are related to motor vehicle crashes, falls, sports, accidents, and abuse or assault.

More than one million children sustain head injuries annually; approximately 165,000 require hospitalization. The National Head Injury Foundation calls TBI "the silent epidemic" because many children have no visible impairments following a head injury. Symptoms can vary greatly, depending upon the extent and location of the brain injury.

Children who sustain TBI may experience a complex array of learning problems including:

Physical impairments
- speech, vision, hearing, and other sensory impairments
- lack of fine-motor coordination, spasticity of muscles, paralysis on one or both sides of the body
- headaches, seizure disorders, balance and gait impairments

Cognitive impairments
- short- and long-term memory deficit, impaired concentration, slowness of thinking, limited attention span
- impairments of perception, communication, reading and writing skills, planning, sequencing, judgment

Psycho-social, behavioral, or emotional impairments
- fatigue, denial, self-centeredness, depression, sexual dysfunction
- lowered self-esteem, lack of motivation, inability to cope, agitation, anxiety, restlessness
- difficulty with emotional control, mood swings, excessive laughing or crying
- inability to self-monitor, difficulty relating to others

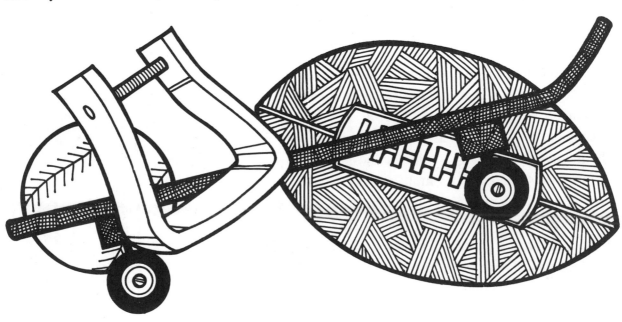

CAUSES AND STRATEGIES FOR LEARNING DISABILITIES

Researchers are still expanding what is known about the causes of learning disabilities. Here are some general observations:

Some children who are considered normal may
- develop and mature at a slower rate than others in the same age group and, as a result, not be able to do expected assignments
- have normal vision and hearing but misinterpret everyday sights and sounds because of some unexplained disorder of the nervous system
- experience an injury or impairment in the womb or at birth that can account for later learning problems (lack of oxygen is one common cause of learning differences)
- have been born prematurely or with some type of medical problem that is responsible for learning delays or disabilities
- have a genetic tendency (the fact that learning disabilities tend to run in families and may be inherited is an area under current study and research)

Boys tend to have a higher rate of learning disabilities than girls. This may be due to the fact that boys tend to mature more slowly than girls.

Children with developmental delays may
- have a limited range of play skills or may play without a purpose
- need more time to imitate and practice play skills
- experience difficulty with any activity requiring abstract thinking
- have difficulty initiating independent activities

Children with learning, emotional, or behavioral difficulties may
- use aggressive behavior, such as hitting, biting, and noise making
- misuse and destroy play or learning materials
- have very short attention spans and exhibit disorganized play activity

Strategies for Adults
- Use positive reinforcement, a highly effective technique.
- Be alert for times when a child is behaving appropriately so you can provide verbal encouragement.
- Use logical consequences as effective guidance controls.
- Maintain consistent daily routines and expectations — a must!
- Use materials that allow for multi-sensory, hands-on experiences.
- Use open-ended activities to encourage imitation and free exploration.
- Stress familiar activities such as games and learning center activities.
- Physically direct a child to complete an activity.
- Break down tasks into smaller increments.

COMPARISON CHART: LEARNING DISABLED AND BRAIN-INJURED STUDENTS

Learning Disabled	TBI (Traumatic Brain Injury)
1. Mild memory problems	1. Severe short-term memory disorder with poor carryover of new learning
2. Congenital, prenatal, or early onset	2. Later onset
3. Slow onset	3. Sudden onset
4. Cause may be unclear; often appears when new demands introduced, e.g., school starts	4. Onset caused by external event
5. Central nervous system loss assumed from "soft" signs	5. Neurological impairment identified from "hard" signs as well as "soft" signs
6. No before-after contrast	6. Marked contrast in pre- and post-onset capabilities, both in self view and others' perception
7. Skills and knowledge show "splinter" development or are underdeveloped	7. Some old skills and knowledge remain but with peaks and valleys of performance
8. Physical disability most likely to involve poor coordination.	8. Physical disability likely to involve paresis (weakness) or spasticity (over-tension)
9. Magnitude of deficits ranges from mild to severe	9. Degree and number of deficits range from mild to severe; often combine to produce severe disability
10. Source of deficits is not necessarily disrupted cognition	10. Deficits based in disrupted cognition
11. Slowed acquisition, but what is learned stays in; teach through strengths and weaknesses	11. Slowed acquisition and what is learned may not stay; needs much repetition and practice using compensatory strategies
12. Status changes comparatively slowly	12. Status changes based on recovery; course may be irregular but improving (rapidly so on initial recovery from coma)
13. Visual perceptual difficulties, often without specific visual impairment	13. Visual perceptual difficulties, often with such visual deficits as double vision and partial loss of vision
14. Distractibility poorly defined and associated with external conditions	14. Distracted by internal thoughts and events as well as external ones
15. No coma	15. Coma produces generalized slowing and lethargy
16. No anti-seizure medications with dulling side effects	16. Cognitive-dulling seizure medications used for prevention in survivors who may never have seizures
17. Recognizes learning deficits	17. Inability to recognize post-injury deficits
18. Behavior modification strategies effective	18. Organic brain dysfunction as well as memory loss may decrease successful use of behavior modification strategies
19. Despite memory problems, new learning can be linked with past learning	19. Linkage of new learning to past experiences may be impeded by loss of old (remote) memory
20. Emotionally prone to outbursts connected to situation	20. Emotions unpredictable; often do not match situation

HOW DO YOU LEARN?

What You Do

Use the following letters to agree or disagree with the statements below. Write the letters in the blanks provided.

Y = yes   **N = no**   **S = sometimes**

_____ When the teacher is talking, I blurt out answers.

_____ I have trouble waiting for my turn.

_____ I love to talk and do it even when I'm supposed to be quiet.

_____ I like to risk and take a chance when riding my bike.

_____ I like to play very quietly, usually by myself.

_____ I enjoy jumping from task to task without completing the first one.

_____ Following oral directions is always easy for me to do.

_____ I always stay in my assigned seat.

_____ Outside noises capture my interest; I can tell you what is happening.

_____ I never interrupt my teacher or classmates.

_____ I can always find my book or pencil when I need it.

_____ I find that I cannot keep my mind on what the teacher is saying.

_____ I need to move my body all the time, fidgeting or squirming in my seat.

_____ I enjoy listening to the teacher. I can do this for a long time.

_____ I can remember all the jobs the teacher or an adult gives me at one time.

_____ I notice that I can be happy one minute and very sad the next minute.

_____ I am unhappy when there is a change in the daily schedule.

_____ I drop my pencil, papers, or books often. I can't help it.

_____ I have difficulty making up my mind.

_____ I am always one of the last students to finish my worksheets.

_____ In my mind, I skip or hop very well. When I try it with my body, I can't do it.

_____ I wish I could do better on tests.

_____ I wish I had more friends.

_____ I get upset with myself because I get angry often and easily.

• Underline the things you said yes to. Then ask your teacher for positive ideas about your behavior in class. Ask your teacher to describe the ways you learn best. List them below.

_____

_____

_____

_____

ARE YOU UP OR DOWN?

People have many different feelings or emotions each day. What emotion might you feel when . . .

- the teacher calls on you to read aloud?   _____
- your work is not finished and time is up?   _____
- you are the first to complete an assignment?   _____
- everyone agrees with your opinion?   _____

What You Do
Complete the expression on each face to match the emotion written under the face.

HAPPY   TIRED   TENSE   CALM   EXCITED

MAD   SICK   CONFUSED   SCARED   FRUSTRATED

PROUD   GROUCHY   SHOCKED   SILLY   SAD

WHAT'S YOUR REACTION?

In a sentence or two, describe a situation you have experienced at school. The class will try to come up with a one-word description and facial expression to describe how you felt in that situation.

Examples

The teacher called on me when I didn't know the answer.

The principal overheard my conversation about how awful the cafeteria food is.

What Happened? Building Empathy

Discuss with a friend or your class what might have happened to make a person . . .

angry or pleased
excited or depressed
shocked or peaceful
glad or gloomy
contented or dismayed

AREN'T YOU FINISHED YET?

Purpose: To allow more able children to experience firsthand some of the frustrations frequently experienced by classmates with learning disabilities when they are forced to work under pressure or against unreasonable deadlines

Note: Timing is important for this activity. When timed correctly, it helps all children understand and appreciate individual differences.

What You Need
- a math worksheet for your age level or group, one copy for each participant (see page 80)
- a timer with a bell or other audible signal (preferably one that ticks loudly)
- pencils for all participants

What You Do
1. Hand a worksheet face down to each student.
2. Caution students not to turn over their papers until you tell them to begin.
3. Explain to students that they will be working against time and will have to work as quickly as possible. Be emphatic. Create a feeling of urgency.
4. Set the timer for half the time you think most class members will need to complete the worksheet.
5. Tell students to turn over their papers and begin.
6. As students work, alternately ask how many have finished or tell them how little time they have left. Every now and then, ask in an exasperated and incredulous tone, "Aren't you finished yet?"
7. When the timer sounds, tell students to stop work immediately, put down their pencils, and turn over their papers.
8. Ask those who finished to raise their hands.
9. Ask those who did not finish to raise their hands.
10. Express surprise. In a tone of disbelief, ask a few specific students why they did not finish.
11. Pause for a moment. Then confess that the exercise was not really fair. Explain that you intentionally allowed students less time than you thought they would need and that you kept nagging them about time so they would have trouble concentrating.

What You Say
   After you explain the exercise, encourage students to be honest about how they felt while doing it. Help them understand that people work at different paces. Some children, especially those with learning differences, need more time to complete assignments.

Ask
- Did you feel pressured and frustrated?
- How would you feel if you thought you could never finish your work on time?
- Would you keep trying anyway?

MATH SKILLS WORKSHEET

What You Do

Work the problems below as quickly as you can. This is a timed test. You must finish in the time allowed.

	a	b	c	d	e
1	0 + 0	5 − 2	3 + 6	5 0 + 1	4 3 + 2
2	42 + 7	65 + 14	37 + 11	56 + 2	103 + 25
3	4 + 3	92 + 1	45 − 21	42 13 + 50	14 91 + 4
4	45 + 21	29 − 18	75 + 8	23 − 3	32 24 + 40
5	75 + 11	44 + 19	44 − 19	17 10 + 41	34 43 + 13
6	75 − 21	67 + 43	27 + 38	96 − 84	61 − 15
7	76 − 28	47 − 26	61 − 15	72 + 50	53 + 68

Kids With Special Needs
 ©1996–The Learning Works

MIRROR WRITING

Purpose: To help children understand how confusing perceptual misinterpretation can be

Some individuals with learning differences perceive or see things differently from most people. Their brains have trouble organizing and interpreting visual stimuli. To them, objects in one place may appear to be in another. The lines and shapes that make up letters and numbers may look backwards or reversed.

What You Need
- worksheet with double-line shape on page 82
- a mirror
- a piece of cardboard
- pencils

What You Do
1. Make enough copies of the worksheet on page 82 so that each student can have one.
2. Attach the mirror securely to a board or wall behind a desk or table.
3. Have pencils available.
4. Hold or mount a piece of cardboard so that students working at the desk or table will not be able to see their hands.
5. Tell students to come to the desk one at a time and bring their worksheets.
6. Place each student's worksheet on the desk or table so it is covered by the cardboard and reflected in the mirror.

What You Say
Give the following directions verbally or provide printed copies for students:
1. Look in the mirror, not at your hands.
2. Write your name on the name line at the top of the page.
3. Trace between the lines of the double shape.
4. On the lines at the bottom of the page, write a short message for a friend to read.

Follow-Up Activity
- Ask students how they felt when their hands seemed to go the wrong direction. Help them understand that children with learning differences, for whom drawing and writing are difficult, have similar feelings.

MIRROR WRITING

When the teacher calls your name, take this worksheet to the drawing table. Then follow the instructions the teacher gives you.

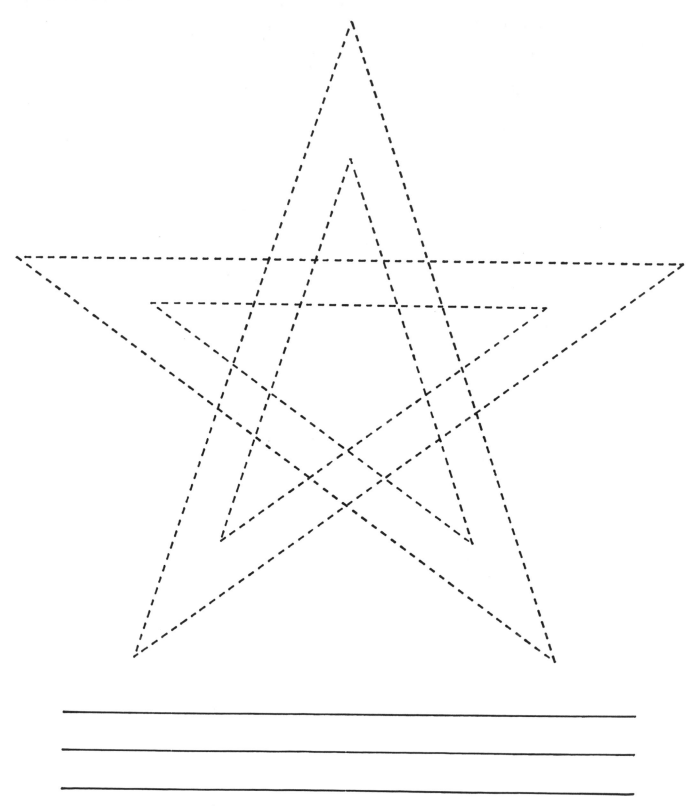

FOLLOW DIRECTIONS

Some children with learning disabilities have trouble understanding what they read and following written directions. Even though they try very hard, they get mixed up and may not be able to do something as fast as other children.

See how well you understand directions. You have three minutes to read and follow the directions on this page.

Name _____

1. Read everything before doing anything.

2. Print your name on the line in the upper right-hand corner of this page.

3. Circle the word name in sentence 2.

4. Draw five small squares in the lower right-hand corner of this page.

5. Put an X in each square.

6. Put a small circle around each square.

7. Sign your name under the title of this page.

8. After the title, write, "yes, yes, yes."

9. Put a circle around sentence number 7.

10. Put an X in the lower left-hand corner of the page.

11. Draw a triangle around this X.

12. On the other side of this paper, add 236 and 435.

13. Draw a circle around the word page in sentence 4.

14. Raise the hand you don't write with and go on to complete number 15.

15. Put your arithmetic book on top of your desk.

16. On the other side of this paper, subtract 79 from 97.

17. Put a circle around your printed name and a square around the circle.

18. Underline all of the even numbers on this page.

19. Say out loud, "I am nearly finished. I have followed directions."

20. Now that you have finished reading carefully, do only the directions in sentences 1 and 2.

GOING ON A TRIP

Purpose: To demonstrate differences in accumulative memory by playing a game based on items that disabled people use

What You Do

Ask students to sit in a circle so that each person has eye contact with everyone else. Designate one person to be the starter. The starter says the following phrase and adds an item someone with a disability might use.

"I'm going on a trip, and because of my disability, I'm taking a very large backpack that contains . . ."

The complete sentence, including the item, is then repeated by the person sitting to the left of the starter, and that person adds another item to the backpack. The extended sentence is passed to the next person, who adds another item, and so on around the circle until someone can't remember what's in the backpack.

Suggestions to Fill the Backpack

protective headgear
knee and elbow pads
a crutch
a leg brace
a pair of glasses
a hearing aid
a computer with an assistive device
a wheelchair
medications
garments with tape-type fastenings
a portable ramp
a walker
special grips for spoons or pencils
a cuddly security item, like a stuffed bear
a guide dog or canine companion
a sighted guide
a lap-top computer
a white cane
a magnifying glass
a phonic ear
a medical alert bracelet

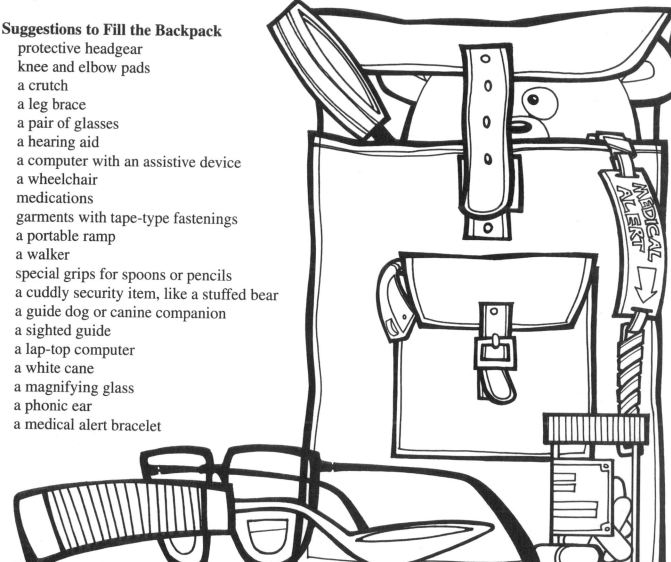

MEMORY GAME

Play this game to assess and sharpen your memorization skills.

What You Need

Assemble the following items on a large tray suitable for passing around a circle of students. Cover th tray with a cloth to prevent sneak previews.

- plastic toy dog
- pair of glasses
- set of ear plugs purchased at a hardware store
- computer disk
- protective helmet
- ID bracelet or medical alert emblem

- chopstick painted white
- hearing aid
- pill bottle
- special cup with two handles
- black felt-tip pen for large printing
- handicapped access symbol

(If any of these items are not available, you can draw replicas on index cards.)

What You Do

1. Have students or participants sit in a circle.

2. Place the tray with its cloth covering in the middle of the circle.

3. Take the cloth off the tray and allow all students to view the tray for one to two minutes. Cover the tray again.

4. Ask students to write down the items they recall seeing on the tray.

5. Name all twelve items and explain each item's connection to a disability.

To make the game harder, ask each student to write down both the item and the disability or need to which it is connected. For example: The handicapped access symbol indicates a parking space for the disabled; a plastic toy dog indicates a guide dog for the legally blind person.

SQUIGGLES AND LINES DO MAKE AN ALPHABET

Learning to read is like breaking a code. Each squiggle or letter stands for a sound. Children who are learning disabled have trouble remembering what sounds go with what letters. Some children are confused about whether to read the white spaces or the black lines. Think about it. How did you learn to read?

The following is a new alphabet. It's made up of different squiggles and lines.

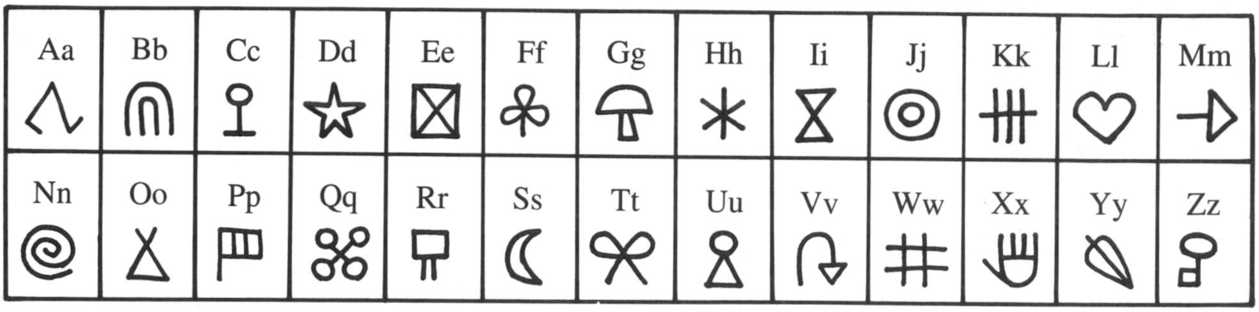

Aa
Bb
Cc
Dd
Ee
Ff
Gg
Hh
Ii
Jj
Kk
Ll
Mm
Nn
Oo
Pp
Qq
Rr
Ss
Tt
Uu
Vv
Ww
Xx
Yy
Zz

Message:

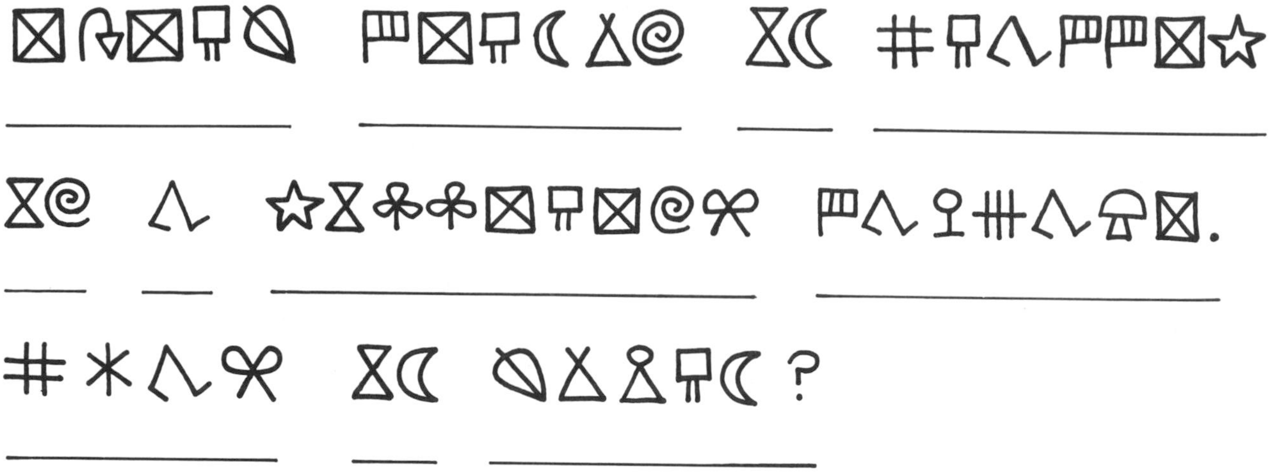

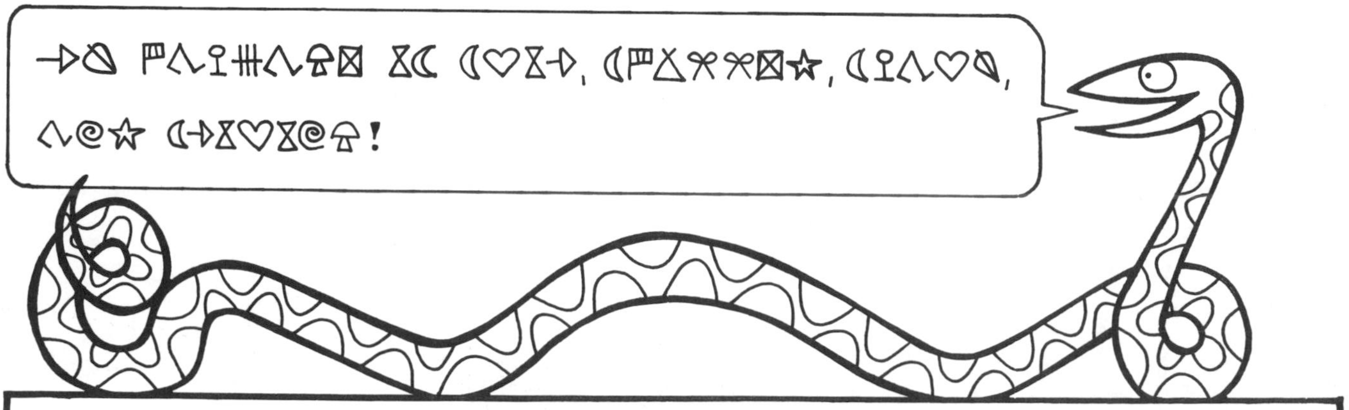

Answer: Every person is wrapped in a different package. What is yours?

TRY IT!

Purpose: To provide experiences that simulate disabilities

What You Do

The following activities simulate different disabilities. Choose one or more for students to try. Give instructions orally, or write out the instruction for each activity you decide to use.

What You Need

Materials will vary depending on the activities you choose. You can also use these activities for the Obstacle Course on page 52.

What Students Do

1. Peel a potato with only one hand. (physical/small motor disability)

2. Walk on crutches or climb stairs using only one leg. (physical/orthopedic disability)

3. Looking through the wrong end of a pair of binoculars, follow a string that has been strung around the room. (visual impairment and perceptual disability)

4. With a friend, walk blindfolded around the school campus, into elevators, up the stairs, and over different surfaces like grass, asphalt, etc. (visual impairment)

5. Thread a needle while wearing two pairs of rubber gloves. (physical/fine-motor disability)

6. Put on a shirt and button it while wearing two pairs of rubber gloves. (physical/fine-motor disability)

7. Write your name on a piece of paper by looking only in a mirror. (learning disability)

8. With one leg and arm strapped down and immobile, sit in a wheelchair and try to get around the room or school setting for about 30 minutes. (physical disability)

9. Write your name by holding the pencil in your mouth. Write your name by holding the pencil between your toes. (physical disability)

10. Throw a ball in the air and catch it. Now close one eye and throw the ball again, catching it with your nondominant hand. (visual impairment)

11. With your finger, draw a letter on the sole of a friend's foot and have the person try to guess it. Now rub the person's sole with a terry-cloth towel and repeat the process. What did your friend notice? (tactile sensitivity)

12. Decode a message using the alphabet on page 86. Time yourself. (learning differences)

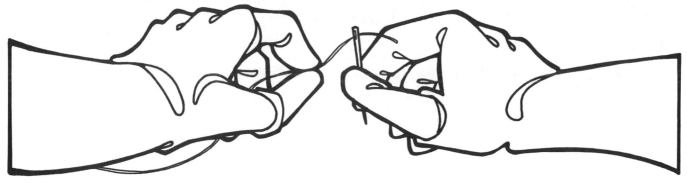

CAN YOU FOLLOW THESE DIRECTIONS?

Some children with learning disabilities have trouble understanding what they read because their brains mix up the letters.

The letters in the directions below are already mixed up. Your brain will have to straighten them out. You have three minutes to read each sentence carefully and do what it says.

1. Print your name in capital letters in the upper right-hand corner of a piece of paper.

2. Underneath it, draw a circle that is 3 inches in diameter.

3. In the middle of the page, draw a square that measures 6 inches on each side.

4. When you have finished, raise your hand.

YOU'RE A STAR!

Purpose: To provide students with an experience that demonstrates a fine-motor or perceptual disability

What You Need
- an assortment of different-size stars drawn with various widths of black lines
- scissors (you'll need several pairs of left-handed scissors)
- colored construction paper
- glue

What You Do
1. Instruct students to cut out the stars and glue them onto sheets of construction paper.
2. Make sure every student uses his or her nondominant hand to cut out and glue the stars.

After the project is finished, ask:
- Are you pleased with your work?

- Is your work as good as you would like it to be?

- How do you think students with perceptual problems feel when their work is not as good as they would like it to be?

POTPOURRI OF PUZZLES

Purpose: To provide opportunities to distinguish a part of a picture from the entire picture

What You Need
- foam board purchased from a craft supply store
- glue stick
- pictures from magazines or pictures that children have drawn
- clear adhesive-backed paper
- precision knife or razor (for adult use only)

What You Do
1. Cut pieces of foam board that are about half an inch larger than each picture you wish to mount.

2. Glue each picture to its foam board.

3. Cover the picture and foam board with clear adhesive paper.

4. Cut the picture into puzzle pieces. Be sure the difficulty of the pieces matches the level of the child. (For example: a three-year-old child starts with puzzles of five to seven pieces; a five-year-old child may have advanced to twelve to fifteen pieces.)

5. Store puzzles in zip-lock bags to prevent mixing pieces. The back of the puzzle pieces can be coded by number, letter, or color to help with sorting if two or more puzzles get mixed together.

Children enjoy puzzles that coordinate with favorite books or units of study.

Puzzles as Gifts

This activity can be used at gift-giving time. Students can draw or bring to class pictures they want to use for puzzles. Older students may be able to assemble their own puzzles as gifts.

SENSORY AWARENESS: USING ALL MODALITIES

Our brains gain information through our senses. This is the learning ladder for all six senses.

Visual – sight
Auditory – hearing
Tactile – touch
Kinesthetic – internal muscle sensations
Olfactory – smell
Gustatory – taste

Different parts of the brain have different jobs. If a certain part is damaged, the ability to see, hear, move, think, or taste may be affected.

When children have trouble learning something, it may help them to use as many of their senses as they can. If they still can't learn something, they should try using one sense lower on the learning ladder.

A Fruitful Experience

Purpose: To provide an overview of how the brain gets information

What You Need
Bring to class an attractive display of fruits, such as blueberries, oranges, lemons, bananas, and/or red, yellow, and green apples.

What You Do
Have each student choose a piece of fruit and examine it in detail, using all six senses. Help each student fill out the chart on the next page. You may want to demonstrate the activity for the entire group.

What You Say
After students have completed their charts, review with them how much information the brain received and stored away for the next time they see or hear about that piece of fruit.

Ask
- What would your life be like if some of this information were missing?
- What if you couldn't remember your fruit unless you saw it? Unless you touched it?

This experience simulates what it is like for a TBI victim to live with memory loss.

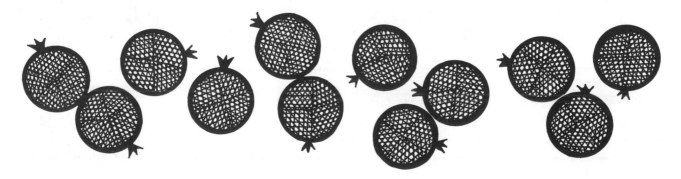

A FRUITFUL EXPERIENCE

Our brains gather information through our senses. Here is the learning ladder for our six senses.

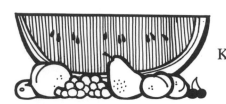

Visual – sight
Auditory – hearing
Tactile – touch
Kinesthetic – internal muscle sensations
Olfactory – smell
Gustatory – taste

When you have trouble learning something, try using as many of your senses as you can. If learning is still hard, try using the next sense down on the ladder of six senses.

What You Do

Choose a piece of fruit and examine it in detail, using all six senses. For your fruit, make a chart like the one below. Ask yourself the following questions when you experience your fruit.

Visual – sight
  When you look at your fruit, what colors, lines, shapes, and markings do you see?

Auditory – hearing
  What are the sounds you hear when you peel or bite into your fruit?   SQUISH!

Tactile – touch
  When you pick up your fruit, what is the texture of its skin?

Kinesthetic – internal muscle sensations
  Is your fruit squishy or firm? Is it heavy or light?

Olfactory – smell
  What aroma or smell does your fruit have?

Gustatory – taste
  How does your fruit taste? (sweet, tart, sour, spicy, bland, etc.)

Kids With Special Needs
©1996–The Learning Works

JOURNAL ENTRIES AND RECALL

Purpose: To allow students to experience the feeling of a memory loss disability

What You Need
- a journal for each student

What You Do
1. After students have been back from lunch for an hour, ask them to take out their journals and enter the time, date, and place. Then ask them to describe in detail exactly what they had for lunch that day:
   - types of food
   - size of the portions
   - tastes they enjoyed

2. Have students put away their journals when they are finished.

3. Several days later, have students form pairs and exchange information about what they recall eating on the day recorded in their journals. Each student should try to describe exactly what he or she had for lunch. The partner looks at the journal record and compares what is recalled to what was recorded.

4. Lead a discussion that includes the following questions and the primary point to be learned:
   - How much did you remember without checking your journal? Most? Half? Very little?
   - What kinds of things did you remember?
   - Why do you think you remembered those things? (For example, the food was especially bad, a favorite food was served, something unusual happened, etc.)
   - The memory is a powerful learning tool, and there are ways to increase its efficiency.

Follow-Up Activity
Compare the experience of average students to that of a student with head trauma and learning impairments.

WHAT'S MISSING?

Directions: Have students study picture A for three minutes. Collect all the copies of picture A. Distribute picture B and ask students to list as many of the missing items as they can. Set a time limit appropriate for your students' grade or age.

A

B

Answer: The camel, fish, mouse, owl, penguin, rabbit, seal, and toucan are missing.

CHAPTER 4
COMMUNICATION DISABILITIES

INTRODUCTION

Communication skills provide vital connections to the learning and understanding process. Learning to listen, speak clearly, follow directions, and repeat information correctly are key accomplishments for every student, regardless of age. The main way a child communicates is with his or her voice. Before a child can learn language, the child needs to be able to hear what is being said.

It is often difficult for a parent or teacher to recognize the signs of poor hearing. Children who do not "sound as if they are trying to talk" by the time they reach their first birthday should be examined by a qualified ear specialist (otologist or otolaryngologist). For a minor, undetected hearing problems can camouflage a child's true personality. Frequently, a child who has been regarded as "slow," "inattentive," "refusing to participate in group activities," or "mumbling words" may in fact be suffering from a different problem — defective hearing.

This chapter provides many opportunities to experience what it would be like to have a hearing loss.

COMMUNICATION DISABILITIES

Children with hearing or communication disabilities . . .
- may have difficulty understanding directions and routines
- may have limited communication with other children and may interfere with their play
- may act out due to frustration with their inability to be understood
- may demonstrate a lack of attention
- may lack appropriate or expected speech development
- may have difficulty making themselves understood
- may lack the language skills to initiate or enter into play or learning situations
- may have difficulty following directions
- may use limited vocabulary

Teaching Strategies
- Heighten children's awareness of all sensory input: touch, smell, taste, hearing, and vision.

- Make sure that all children are able to see you at all times.

- Check to see that students are on the correct page in workbooks.

- Get the child's attention before talking to him or her. Use phrases such as "Jason, please look at me."

- Use tactile and visual clues throughout the environment. Examples are flashing lights, pictures to give directions, bold labels, and various textures.

- Assign a student helper to notify the child in emergency situations when bells may sound, such as fire drills, disaster drills, etc.

- Have the child work in small group settings.

- Provide clear language models for all children.

- Use comments such as "show me" to help the child communicate. Give the child words to use, such as, "I'm your friend, Anna, and I want to play with your toy."

- Use simple vocabulary with short, easy-to-understand sentences.

- Listen attentively to each child and maintain eye contact.

- Provide many opportunities for all children to express themselves and to listen with respect to others.

Kids With Special Needs
©1996–The Learning Works

SETTING THE STAGE FOR LISTENING

Purpose: To demonstrate to children that rules are needed so that communications can be clearly understood and each person's ideas listened to and heard

What You Need
- cassette tape recorder and tape
- a very noisy listening time

What You Do
1. Record the racket and noise level of a disorganized circle or group time.

2. The next day, ask the children to sit in a circle on the floor or in chairs so that each person can look at everyone else. Call the group to order and state the problem.

3. Ask students to listen to how they sounded the previous day. Play the tape.

4. Ask students how they felt while they listened and what suggestions they have to make listening time a better time for listening, thinking, and sharing.

5. Write all ideas on a large piece of paper or the chalkboard. The group may wish to vote on the list. The fewer the rules, the easier it is for children to remember and comply with them.

6. You may wish to talk about everyone's right to hear, and to discuss the importance of respecting and accepting all individuals.

7. Post a final copy of the rules.

8. Evaluate the rules at the end of each day until they have become habits in your classroom. Remember, it takes two weeks to six months for a habit to form. Be patient. Use positive statements of encouragement.

Follow-Up Activities
- Have children copy the list of rules on a separate piece of paper to use as a book cover.

- Post a different student's list each day as a reminder to the entire group that the focus will be on respectful listening. Have that student conduct the evaluation at the end of the day. Thank the student for taking care of this task.

- Create a graph and record the results on a daily basis. Select a different student to fill in the graph each day.

DECIBELS

Noise can be measured in units called decibels. The greater the number of decibels, the louder the noise. Most of the sounds you hear every day measure between 30 and 80 decibels. If you listen for a long time to sounds louder than 85 decibels, your hearing may be harmed or impaired.

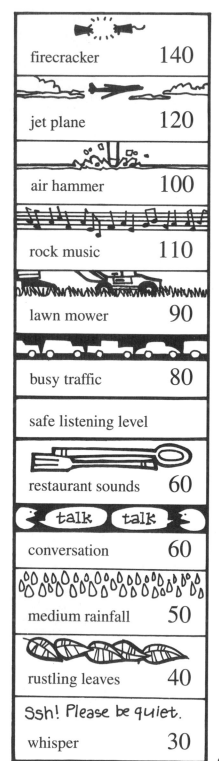

firecracker	140
jet plane	120
air hammer	100
rock music	110
lawn mower	90
busy traffic	80
safe listening level	
restaurant sounds	60
conversation	60
medium rainfall	50
rustling leaves	40
Ssh! Please be quiet. whisper	30

OUCH! NOISE POLLUTION

What You Do

1. Cut apart the following pictures and sort them into two categories — safe, pleasant sounds, and sounds that cause noise pollution.

2. Paste the examples of noise pollution inside the frame and the safe sounds outside the frame.

3. Discuss with your classmates how to cut down noise pollution or how to protect your ears from loud noise.

Remember: If you can't carry on a conversation in the presence of a noise, the noise is too loud for your ears and may cause hearing loss.

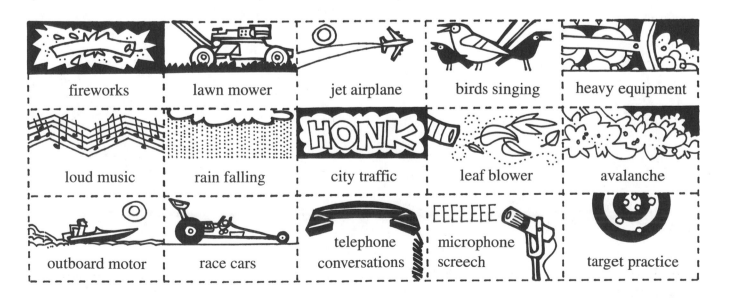

fireworks	lawn mower	jet airplane	birds singing	heavy equipment
loud music	rain falling	city traffic	leaf blower	avalanche
outboard motor	race cars	telephone conversations	microphone screech	target practice

HEARING IMPAIRMENTS

Hearing impairments affect two out of every one hundred school children.

Hearing impairments can be **caused** by:
- the aging process
- birth defects
- certain drugs
- ear wax
- head trauma or head injuries
- heredity
- middle ear infections
- prolonged or repeated exposure to loud noises
- tumors
- viral infections

Some hearing impairments can be **prevented** by:
- avoiding loud noises whenever possible
- having your hearing tested periodically
- not putting anything smaller than your elbow into your ear
- seeing a doctor when your ear aches
- wearing hearing protectors when you must work or play near loud noise
- wearing protective headgear when there is some danger that your head may be bumped or hit while you work or play

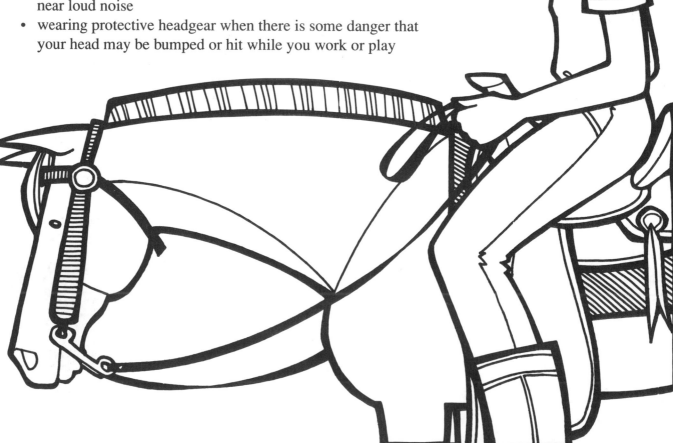

HEARING AIDS

Many people with hearing impairments can benefit from using hearing aids. Hearing aids amplify sounds, making them louder and easier to hear. There are several kinds of hearing aids. Some are worn on the body. Some are worn in or near the ear. All hearing aids are powered by batteries and have tiny microphones to collect sounds. They have switches so the wearer can control the volume of the sound he or she hears.

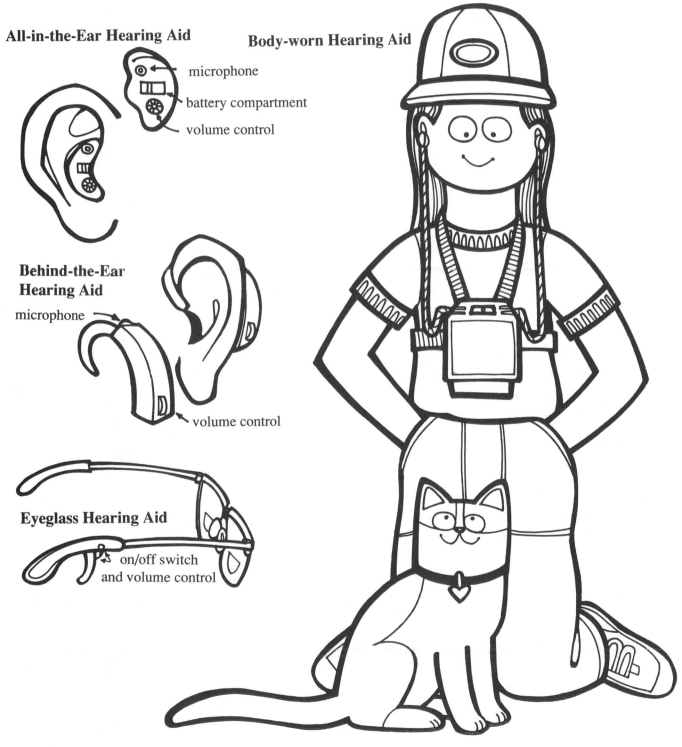

All-in-the-Ear Hearing Aid

microphone

battery compartment

volume control

Body-worn Hearing Aid

Behind-the-Ear Hearing Aid

microphone

volume control

Eyeglass Hearing Aid

on/off switch and volume control

LISTEN AND HEAR

Purpose: To help children become aware of the ways in which a hearing loss interferes with communication and may affect academic learning

What You Need
- cotton balls
- foam ear plugs from a hardware store (one pair for each student)
- swimmers' ear plugs
- personalized ear plugs made especially to fit each child
- ear phones

What You Do
Ask the group the following questions:
- What do all these objects have in common?
- How are they used?
- Why might your ears need protection?
  - to prevent infections
  - to prevent possible hearing loss

Activity 1
1. Read the following paragraph in a normal voice. *"There are many types of educational programs for children with hearing impairments. Some children with a hearing impairment need help from resource teachers and/or speech and language specialists. Many things affect the ability of a child who is hearing impaired to do well in school. Among them are the degree and type of loss and the child's intelligence and motivation."*

2. Have students put their hands over their ears or use their pair of foam ear plugs. Then read the paragraph again. Talk about how the sound is muffled. (A conductive hearing loss is common in school-age children.)

3. Read the paragraph again with your hand or a handkerchief over your mouth. Again, talk about how the sound is muffled or distorted. (A sensorineural hearing loss means a child hears at a lower level with distortion.)

Activity 2
Have the class listen to a radio station that has a weak signal characterized by static. (Improperly fitted or damaged hearing aids may emit static like this.)

Activity 3
Discuss some of the difficulties involved in communicating when you have a hearing loss.

Activity 4
Read and discuss the poem by Jeanne Maree Iacono on pages 198-199.

OUTSPOKEN SPEECHES

Purpose: To help children become aware of the frustrations faced by classmates who need to work with a speech or language specialist

What You Do
1. Read the following examples to the class, one at a time.
2. After you read each example, discuss both the listener's and the speaker's feelings during communication. Emphasize the speaker's frustrations.

Articulation disorder — abnormal production of speech sound
A thpeech dithoda ith not funny. It can be vewy embawathing to the thpeaka. Even a mild dithoda can cauthe a mithunduthtanding.

Language disorder — inability to clearly put thoughts into words or sentences
No make words say right. Can't. Not funny. Talk bad; feel hurt, sad.

Stuttering — the lack of fluency in an individual's speech pattern, often heard as hesitations or repetitions of sounds or words
Aa-a-a-a ssspeech d-d-d-disorder is not f-f-funny. It c-c-can be, uhm, you know, uhm very embaaaarrasing to the-the speaker. Eeeven a m-mild dis-dis-disorder can cause a (cough) mis-mis-mis-misunderstanding.

Voice disorder — poor or unusual voice quality, such as a voice that is hoarse, soft, or too deep
(Whisper hoarsely) A speech disorder is not funny. It can be very embarrassing to the speaker. Even a mild disorder can cause a misunderstanding.

Average speaker
A speech disorder is not funny. It can be very embarrassing to the speaker. Even a mild disorder can cause a misunderstanding.

TALKING THROUGH YOUR TEETH

Speech problems and disabilities have existed since the beginning of time. In ancient times, a famous Greek philosopher, Socrates, struggled with unclear speech. The story that has come down through the ages tells how he filled his mouth with beach pebbles and practiced speaking. This tale can be an inspiration to youngsters with speech difficulties.

Have students be like Socrates and try this activity.

Purpose: To learn how it might feel to have a speech disability

What You Need
- printed reading selection at the proper reading level for this group

What You Do
1. Pass out the duplicated reading selection and have the entire group read it aloud. Discuss any difficult words that may be in the passage.

2. Ask the students to clench their teeth. Have the group read the passage aloud a second time through clenched teeth.

3. Discuss with the students how it felt not to be able to communicate clearly. Laughter and embarrassment are also good topics for discussion.

104

FINGER SPELLING

Some people who cannot hear, learn to spell and speak with their fingers. The alphabet for finger spelling is pictured below.

Use this alphabet. Practice finger spelling your name, a greeting, and a word that describes a feeling.

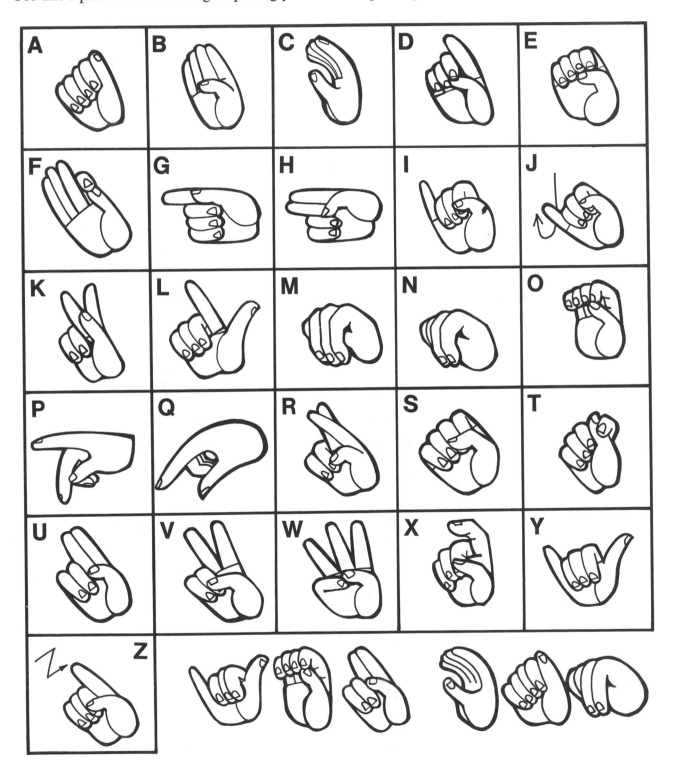

BE A FINGER SPELLING CHAMP

Use the finger spelling alphabet shown on page 105 for these activities.

Spelling Test
- Learn your weekly list of spelling words in two ways so you can spell each word out loud and with finger spelling.

- Ask your teacher to award points for each way that you spell the words. You might earn one point when you spell a word correctly out loud and two points when you use correct finger spelling.

Words about Senses
- Learn to spell the following words using the finger spelling alphabet on page 105.

    seeing
    hearing
    tasting
    smelling
    touching
    feeling
    at least six classmates' names

Kids With Special Needs
©1996–The Learning Works

FINGER SPELLING BINGO GAME

What You Need
- one master set of alphabet letter cards to use for randomly drawing and calling out letters
- one Bingo card per player
- enough markers for each player

What You Do
1. Construct Bingo cards similar to those used in the commercial game, but instead of letters, duplicate and paste the finger alphabet signs from page 105 into the squares on the cards. Make sure every card has a variety of signs and one free space.

2. To play the game, give every student a card and a collection of markers.

3. Call out the letters and have students find any corresponding finger alphabet sign on their cards.

4. For a variation, use regular letters on the Bingo cards, but when you "call" the letters, use the finger alphabet signs. Either form the signs with your hand or hold up a picture of the sign.

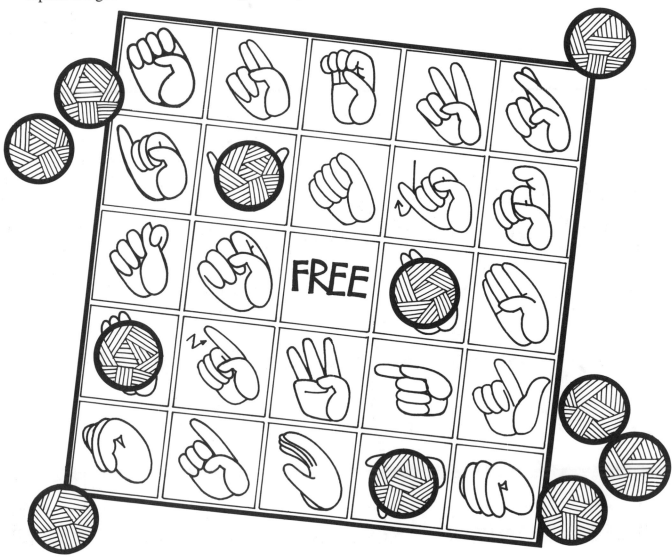

COMMUNICATION DISORDERS

We all enjoy talking with others, even if they — or we — cannot speak. Computer technology provides new ways to communicate. Technology can speak for us! It can offer a synthetic voice for those who can't express their thoughts out loud. Augmentative and alternative communication (AAC) devices can talk for us.

Augmentative communication devices: alternative methods of communicating (such as communication boards, communication books, sign language, and computerized voices)

Communication board: a flat device on which words, pictures, or other symbols are used to expand the verbal interactions of people with limited vocal abilities

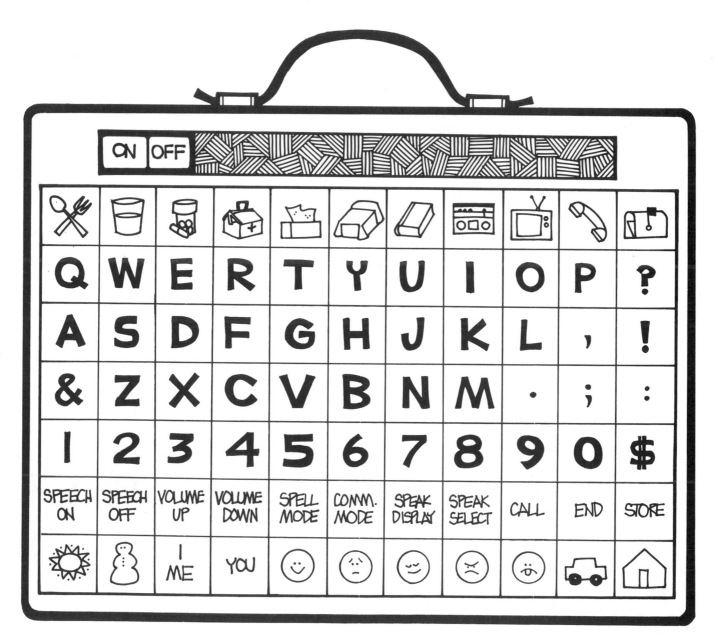

Kids With Special Needs
©1996–The Learning Works

SIMULATIONS TO INCREASE AWARENESS OF HEARING DISABILITIES

- Read a familiar story to the class, but ask students to cover their ears with their hands or with earphones while they listen. Ask questions about the story and discuss what it may be like to be hearing impaired.

- Read a different story to the class without making any sound. Then have the class guess what the story was about. The illustrations of the book you choose will add or subtract to this experience. This simulates a child who lip reads.

- Play a radio loudly. While it plays, give students directions in a low, quiet tone of voice. Discuss the students' reactions and feelings. This experience helps children understand how students with hearing impairments must filter out background noises, even with hearing devices.

- Rent or borrow a captioned video to show to the class. Ask the class for reactions. (For videotape sources, see Chapter 8: Resources and Organizations of Interest.)

- Demonstrate a tuning fork and its similarities to the functions of the ear.

- Purchase a pair of foam ear plugs for each student. Have students try different activities with the ear plugs in and then with the ear plugs out. Be sure to carefully supervise students in the use of earplugs in this and all activities.

Story Time
Choose books and activities from Chapter 7: Bibliotherapy to use during story times.

Tabletop and Manipulative Activities
Have various tabletop activities available in the classroom such as the Finger Spelling Bingo game on page 107.

Values Education
Use the following books and the teacher's resource chapter for ideas.
- *The Value of Giving: The Story of Beethoven*, by Ann Donegan Johnson
- *The Value of Determination: The Story of Helen Keller*, by Ann Donegan Johnson

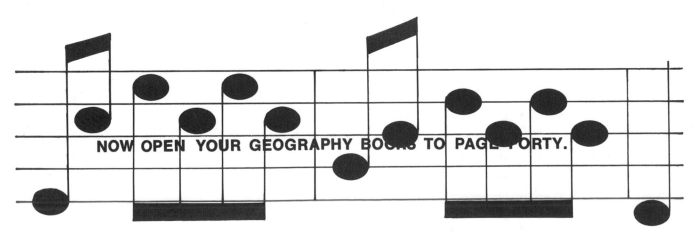

CURRICULUM-RELATED ACTIVITIES

Art

- **Montage:**
Have students cut pictures from magazines and other sources to create a montage of ears surrounded by pictures of things that are interesting to hear. Discuss with your students the sounds that each picture represents.

- **Sculpted sound:**
Have students find examples of sculptures that use sound as part of their artistic effect, like wind chimes and fountains. Have students describe to the class what they found or ask them to bring in pictures or drawings for a classroom display. As an art project, let students construct their own sculptures using bells, hammers, wood blocks, rolling or dropping marbles, etc. You may want to give awards for the most unusual, most inventive, funniest, simplest, most complex, biggest, smallest, most rhythmic, strangest sound, etc.

- **Musical inspiration:**
Put on music for background listening during an art period. Discuss how the music increases creative expression during the art activity.

Language Arts: Drawing and Writing

- After a book discussion, ask children to draw examples of what they would miss hearing most. Have students show their drawings and explain why they would miss the sounds pictured. Ask students to survey their parents and siblings to find out what family members could not hear if they were deaf. Have students write about the sounds family members would miss the most and the problems they would encounter. (See Chapter 7: Bibliotherapy for book titles.)

- Label all objects in the classroom as a learning aid for the hearing-impaired child. Call attention to the importance of signs.

- Have students prepare reports on famous people like Helen Keller, Beethoven, Thomas Edison, etc. Check the list on pages 40-41 for other famous people with a hearing loss.

Music and Movement

- Play a popular song for the class and ask what motions might be used to share the song's words with a person who is hearing impaired. Choose a familiar song and teach the class a sign-language version of the song. Ask the group how each motion portrays the words of the song.

- Take the front off the piano so children can see how and when piano hammers strike to create the different notes. Show a picture of Beethoven and relate a short synopsis of the life of this famous pianist and composer who was hearing impaired.

- Have students perform in a percussion band. Follow the performance with a discussion to point out that hearing-impaired children often enjoy using percussion instruments because they can feel vibrations and see the beat.

CURRICULUM-RELATED ACTIVITIES

Role Playing, Dramatic Play, and Field Trips

- Take students to visit a hearing center so they can become familiar with the various hearing aids available. Allow children who are willing to participate in a hearing test to do so. Have a hearing professional stress safety tips to prevent hearing loss. Go back to the classroom and create a storefront to role-play the experience.

- Have an interpreter come to class to demonstrate and teach simple signs. Learn the finger alphabet.

- Create a game show of safety signs. Use a set of teacher-made signs or a commercially purchased set. Designate a child to be the game show host and to ask different contestants to identify the signs' meanings.

- Invite a local person with a hearing impairment to make a classroom visit.

- Invite an airplane mechanic to share various aspects of the job and the tools used to prevent hearing loss. Ask your guest to demonstrate the hand signals used to direct the plane's pilot.

Graphing

- Create a graph based on the drawing activity for familiar sounds students would miss the most (see Language Arts, page 110). The graph should show which sounds would be missed by students and/or their family members.

Science

- Fill pairs of identical containers (film canisters, plastic margarine tubs, or plastic eggs) with measured amounts of substances such as dried beans, cornmeal, gravel, paper clips, etc. Tape the filled containers shut with sturdy duct tape. Invite children to shake the containers and pair the ones that sound the same. Have them try to identify the contents by sound alone. Have a self-checking poster available for students to check their answers. After all children have identified the contents, create additional containers and self-checking lists.

- Use cassette tapes or prerecorded sound tracks of environmental sounds. From teachers' supply stores, obtain and play a "guess this sound" tape. Have children match the sounds with photos or pictures or create a poster to go with each sound.

- Make play telephones using string and tubes.

- Ask the class to bring in samples of different bells. Facilitate a discussion on the sounds, pitches, and functions of different types of bells. Construct a model of a doorbell with materials purchased at the hardware store: wire, switch, batteries, and an electric bell.

- Look in a science book under the heading *sound* for more classroom activities, such as a demonstration on vibrations, echoes, etc.

GUIDELINES TO HELP THE CHILD WHO IS HEARING IMPAIRED

Children with hearing impairments do not get a chance to "overhear" directions that adults are giving to other children with normal hearing ability. It is important for adults who work with children with hearing impairments to make an extra effort to provide adequate auditory stimulation so that these children's auditory perceptions have a chance to develop.

1. **Do not touch a hearing-impaired child to get his or her attention.**
   If you speak to the child first, he or she will become conditioned to attend to your voice as a signal. If you act as though you do not expect the child to hear, he or she will become conditioned not to listen.

2. **Keep within fairly close range of the child.**
   Sound decreases in power rapidly if the speaker is more than six to ten feet away from the child's hearing aid. For good sound reproduction, stay close to the child and speak in a normal, conversational tone.

3. **Do not stress visual clues if you wish to teach auditory skills.**
   Cover your mouth, if necessary, in order to direct the child's attention to the sound of the words you wish him or her to learn. Routinely sitting beside or slightly behind the child also directs the child to develop listening skills.

4. **Provide adequate auditory stimulation with many repetitions of the auditory patterns you wish the child to learn.**
   For a child to perceive the auditory patterning, the pattern must be repeated many times in a variety of contexts. This means that practice time should provide ample opportunities for the child to listen for the new words, phrases, or sentence patterns you wish to teach.

5. **Give the child time to respond.**
   Listening is temporal and requires auditory processing within the brain. Don't rush an answer if you feel the child should get it without help. On the other hand, if the child has trouble maintaining attention on what he or she has heard, guide the child to the correct response and then repeat the word (or phrase) again.

CHAPTER 5
PHYSICAL DISABILITIES

INTRODUCTION

Children come in all sizes and shapes. Physical disabilities related to size and appearance are often a child's most obvious characteristic. Children who are too short, too tall, too thin, or too heavy stand out in a group.

The cycle of gathering and assimilating information may start when the child is an infant and parents are faced with questions about size and shape. When the child is old enough to answer questions, he or she becomes a spokesperson for that particular disability. When these children reach school age, they will interact with classmates who need information. Teachers of these children must find positive ways of sharing that information with the class.

This chapter provides simple explanations and activities that address physical impairments, including height, vision, and orthopedic disabilities.

Children with physical disabilities . . .
- may have difficulty reaching or handling learning materials
- may be physically unable to participate in an activity
- may be less interested or less motivated to participate

Teaching Strategies
- Provide colorful toys and learning materials that make use of cause and effect.

- Provide physical assistance to give children access to materials.

- Modify activities to allow every child to participate to the fullest extent possible.

WE ALL COME IN DIFFERENT SIZES

Being very small or very large can be a physical disability because so many of the things we wear and use are made for people who are of average size. People who are unusually small, unusually tall, or unusually large often have trouble buying clothes, cars, and furniture. Nothing really seems to fit.

Being very small or very tall may be a hereditary condition. It is not a disease. It is not contagious. A small or tall person may have parents of average size. Small parents or tall parents may have children of average size.

Some people who are very small or short are called little people, or people of short stature. There are two kinds of little people. A midget has normal proportions but is short. A dwarf has a regular-sized body but short arms and legs.

114

WHAT DOES IT FEEL LIKE TO BE SHORT OR TALL?

Activity: Measure each child

Many little people are fewer than 48 inches tall when fully grown and can be as short as twenty-four inches. Many tall people are over six feet. Mark a door frame in twelve- and six-inch increments. Measure each child and write his or her name beside the measurement.

- What does it feel like to be a little person? Go through your house on your knees.
- Can you reach light switches and faucets?
- Can you see things on countertops and tables?

Now stand on a chair and look at the same things from a different height. Move the chair around the room to various locations and take a different look at things you see every day.

Find a series of sturdy boxes in graduated sizes. Measure the height of each box and place that number on the face of the box. Label each box with its height. Help each child add his or her height and the additional height of the box. Now when the child stands on a box, he or she will be able to survey the room in a new perspective — "a heightened awareness."

FAMOUS PERSONALITIES COME IN ALL SIZES

Little people have been big entertainers. They have played important roles on stage, in motion pictures, and on television. The Munchkins in *The Wizard of Oz*, the Oompa-Loompas in *Willy Wonka and the Chocolate Factory*, and the Ewoks in the *Star Wars* series have all been played by little people in special costumes. Children are called "Little Littles" in the Little People of America organization.

Getting Acquainted with Big and Tall People

Very tall people have been star athletes. Basketball is one sport that has featured many tall people over the years.

Some football players and wrestlers have been traditionally very large in body size. Very large people have a disability too. Clothing, furniture, and transportation can present problems for them.

- Older children can create lists of famous personalities and research the careers of these men and women. Writing letters to them with questions pertaining to size being an asset or liability is an interesting exercise, with the possibility of receiving many exciting and unusual replies.

- Investigate career options where being a certain size would be an advantage or disadvantage (jockey, chimney sweep, etc.).

- Hiring criteria for certain professions used to state specific age, weight, and height requirements. This is no longer allowed by federal law. Investigate the law and the court cases that resulted due to unfair hiring or firing practices.

Regardless of size—little or tall—all people can have interesting jobs. They can be architects, authors, engineers, teachers, and musicians. They can be photographers, scientists, and chiropractors—almost anything. In fact, this book was illustrated by a little person, artist Bev Armstrong.

Kids With Special Needs
©1996–The Learning Works

NAMES CAN HURT

Names and stereotypes are often used by the mass media — TV, movies, and magazines. Sometimes these portrayals are amusing because such exaggerations of the real facts make us laugh. In everyday life, when a large person is called "Fatty," it hurts. When a tall person is called "Stretch," it hurts. When a short person is called "Shrimp" or "Peanut," it hurts.

The media relies on the fact that all of us are familiar with certain stereotypes. Can you match the person in the left-hand column to the quality in the right-hand column with which he or she is usually associated?

_____ 1. the elderly	a. are jolly
_____ 2. people with disabilities	b. are absent-minded
_____ 3. teenagers	c. are hot-tempered
_____ 4. redheads	d. are not intelligent
_____ 5. athletes	e. are disrespectful of adults
_____ 6. professors	f. make false promises
_____ 7. midgets/dwarfs	g. are senile
_____ 8. fat people	h. aren't scholars
_____ 9. politicians	i. only read books
_____ 10. librarians	j. only have jobs in the movies

Stereotyping is putting a label on people. Stereotypes distort the truth. They suggest that all people in a particular group behave the same way. It is important to remember that we all have certain characteristics and that no one group has a monopoly on beauty, brains, glamour, strength, humor, or talent.

PUTTING YOUR FEELINGS INTO ACTION

It is important to write or tell TV producers when shows depict stereotypes or people with disabilities in a less than positive view. Standing up and explaining how you feel gives others the courage to do it, too. If writers, announcers, TV newscasters, and radio personalities realize that people care about creating positive images for those with disabilities, they will begin to correct themselves. Make sure that you write or call, giving a compliment when you see or hear something that puts people with disabilities in a positive light.

— talk shows
— TV shows
— commercials
— advertisements featuring models with disabilities

Sample letter from a class

School Letterhead

date
Dear _____ ,

Our class recently had an assignment that required us to watch TV, read newspapers, and listen to the radio to find examples of people with disabilities being role models. This is what we found out about your program [or publication].

State findings:

We applaud the great job you are doing.
or
We are calling this to your attention because it is not fair to any person with a disability.

Please write to us with your thoughts.

Thank you for your time.

grade, school, address, and teacher's name

VITAL VISION

Vision is the richest and most stimulating of our senses. Two-thirds of our information about the outside world comes to us through our eyes. Use the anatomical drawing as a basis for a discussion on the parts of the eye and how it works.

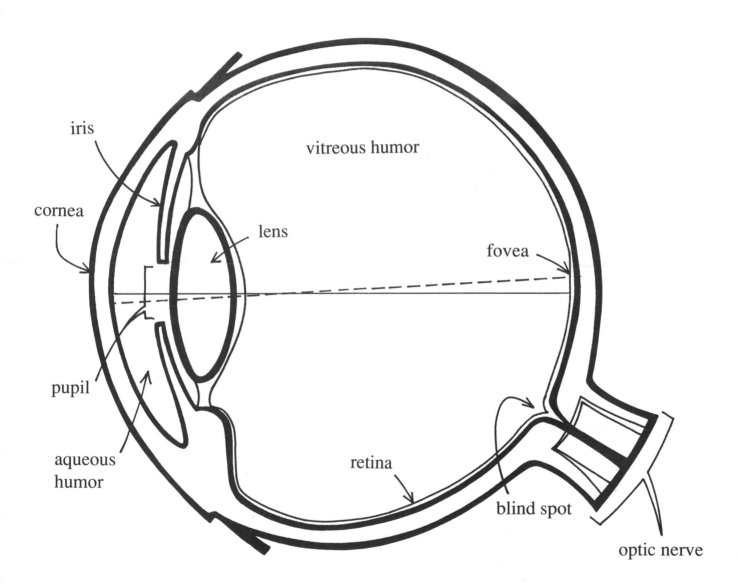

The Human Eye

WHAT CAN A BLIND PERSON SEE?

Visual Impairment:

There are degrees of visual impairment. People who are partially sighted usually have a visual acuity between 20/70 and 20/200 after the best possible correction has been obtained. This means that they see at a distance of twenty feet what a person with unimpaired vision sees at a distance of seventy to two hundred feet. People who are legally blind have less than 20/200 acuity after correction; however, they can see. They are readily able to distinguish light from dark and may also be able to read large print. People who are totally blind often can distinguish light from dark and see large forms.

A youngster may be born with a visual impairment or acquire a visual disability through injury or disease. Youngsters with visual impairments can do almost everything other youngsters can do. At home or in familiar surroundings, they do not need help to find their way around. They rely on memory and on the sense of touch. When they are older they may use a cane, a sighted guide, or a guide dog to help them.

Simulation Activity — Being a Sighted Guide

Directions: Divide the class into pairs. One person elects to be the sighted guide and the other person, visually impaired. Make and use the blindfolds described on page 121. This activity is most effective if it is done for about one to two hours. Put the blindfold on the person choosing to experience a visual impairment. After the time period is up, switch roles with the sighted guide now being visually impaired with the blindfold.

Directions for the Sighted Person

Classroom Investigation

- Direct your partner to hold your arm with his or her thumb and index finger in a V-shape, just above the elbow. As the sighted guide, you should crook your arm and hold it relaxed against your body.

- Walk about one-half step in front of the "blind" person and walk at a normal pace around the classroom. Talk with your partner as you walk, describing the obstacles as you approach them. Continue with your normal school routine, remembering that you are the sighted guide for your partner.

Outdoor Investigation

- Take your partner outdoors to a prepared obstacle course set up by the teacher. If you come to steps, tell your partner if the steps go up or down. If you are going to move to the left or to the right, tell your partner before you do so. Telling your partner in advance about obstacles helps your partner feel more relaxed and safer.

- Approach the narrow passage your teacher has created. Drop your hand down to your side and then behind your back. This signals your partner to go behind you.

Eating a Snack or Lunch

- Describe for your partner the way to pick out the desired foods. Are trays to be carried to the table or will you be served? How is the food arranged on the plate? What are the seating arrangements? Assist your partner.

Discussion Questions:

Is the role of sighted guide as easy as you thought it might be? What was the most difficult part — classroom, outdoors, eating? What emotions did you experience?

Being visually impaired, did you notice that you relied on sounds more? How did the food taste when you were unable to see it? What were your strongest emotions?

INEXPENSIVE, DISPOSABLE BLINDFOLD

This blindfold is
- sanitary
- disposable
- inexpensive
- quick to construct – no sewing needed

For each blindfold the following materials are needed:
- 1 yard of clear or colored plastic food wrap (purchased at the grocery store)
- white liquid glue
- a 10" x 3" strip of fabric
- transparent tape

Directions:
1. Lay the yard of plastic wrap flat on a large work surface.

2. Lightly glue the fabric in the middle of the plastic wrap.

3. Now fold the bottom third of the wrap up and over the glue spot. Fold the top third down. Now gently pat and push the fabric and glue so no wrinkles exist.

4. Apply the wrap snugly over the eyes and pat into place over the bridge of the nose. The ends overlap each other for a tight yet comfortable fit. If you find that the plastic wrap does not adhere securely, use transparent tape.

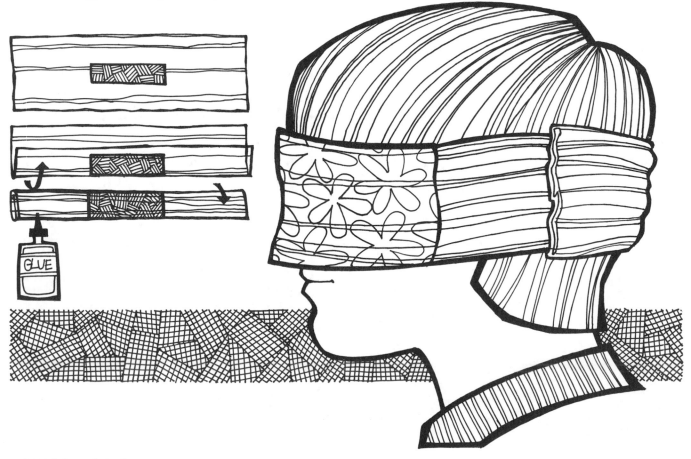

THE BRAILLE ALPHABET

Louis Braille was a French organist and teacher of the blind. He developed a system of raised-dot writing for literature and music. This remarkable system, called the Braille alphabet, makes it possible for people to read with their fingertips, even though they can't see.

The Braille alphabet is based on a rectangle made up of six dot positions. By changing the number of dots used and varying their positions within the rectangle, Louis Braille was able to create enough variations to represent twenty-six letters, ten numerals, and all needed punctuation marks.

Within the rectangle, each dot position has a number. Different combinations of these positions represent different letters, numerals, and punctuation marks and even indicate when a letter should be capitalized. For example, a dot in position 1 represents the letter "a." A combination of dots in positions 2, 5, and 6 stands for a period. A dot in position 6 before a letter indicates that the letter should be capitalized.

HANDS-ON BRAILLE

Purpose: To give children a "hands-on" feel for the Braille alphabet before they write out a Braille message with dots. The only requirement is that the children be able to recognize the alphabet in English.

What You Need for Each Child :
- one-half of an egg carton cut as shown
- 5 cotton balls
- a copy of the alphabet chart on page 122.

It may be helpful to demonstrate or review the following on the chalkboard:

The Braille alphabet is based on a rectangle made up of 6 raised dots.	Each dot position has a number.	Dots in positions 2, 5, and 6 indicate a period.
●● ●● ●●	1 4 2 5 3 6	○ ○ ●● ○ ●

Procedure:

1. Explain to students that instead of dots, they will use cotton balls. The egg carton represents the six positions.

2. Review the numbers of the positions. Have the students print the correct number in the bottom of each egg cup.

3. You may wish to make a set of flash cards showing each letter of the alphabet with empty spaces indicating the positions not used.

    Example: letter a
    ● ○
    ○ ○
    ○ ○

4. Have the class move through the alphabet, practicing the positions of dots by placing cotton balls in their egg cartons.

5. When the process has become familiar, give the class a set of simple words to work on together (for example: me, you, boy, girl, teacher, together, class, sight).

BEASTLY BRAILLE

In the Braille system, each dot position has a number. Each letter can be described by the sequence of numbers that name the positions of the dots used to represent that letter. For example, the letter **c** could be called 1-4, and the letter **z** could be called 1-3-5-6. Use the chart on page 122 to answer the following questions.

1. What number sequence would you use to describe the letter **b**? _____

2. What number would you use to describe the letter **a**? _____

3. What number sequence would you use to describe the letter **t**? _____

4. What series of number sequences would you use to write the word **bat**?

_____ _____ _____

5. Use Braille dots to write the word **bat** in the boxes below.

6. Use Braille dots to write the word **lion** in the boxes below.

7. Use Braille dots to write the word **coyote** in the boxes below.

8. Use Braille dots to write the name of some animal in the boxes below. Then exchange papers with a friend and see if he or she can identify your beast and write its name in letters.

NAMES IN THE NEWS

Purpose: The purpose of this activity is to acquaint children with the Braille alphabet and to make them more aware of newsmakers and current events.

Materials Needed:
- 25 sequentially numbered 3 x 5 index cards with a name written in Braille on each one. (Names should be taken from the newspaper and might include national leaders, political figures, entertainers, sports heroes, and the like.) Cut off the upper right-hand corner of each card so children can tell top from bottom.
- additional blank index cards
- a basket, box, or hat to hold the name cards
- a basket, box, or hat to hold the fact cards
- one copy of the Braille alphabet from page 122 for each child
- paper and pencils

Procedure:
1. Number your paper from 1 through 25.
2. One at a time, take name cards from the container.
3. Identify the letters written in Braille on the card.
4. Note the number on the card, and print your answer on your paper beside that number.
5. When you have identified all of the names, select one name and find out more about the person to whom it belongs. Where was this person born? In what country does this person live? What did he or she do that was newsworthy?
6. For bonus points, write one fact about this person in Braille on one side of a blank index card.
7. Key this fact card to the correct name card by writing the name card number on the other side of the fact card.
8. Put the fact card in the fact card container.

Variations:
- As students read the names written in Braille and print them in letters on their papers, tell them to identify the persons to whom these names belong by office, title, or achievement.

- When the number of fact cards has grown sufficiently large, challenge students to match name cards with fact cards and to check the accuracy of their matches by comparing the numbers on the front of the name cards with those written on the back of the fact cards.

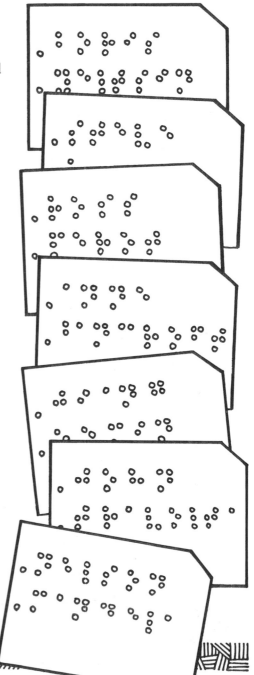

DOTS DO IT!

This activity would be a marvelous follow-up activity after a Braille transcriber has visited the classroom and shown students the type of work he or she does.

Purpose: This activity helps students become better acquainted with the Braille alphabet and lets them practice working in pairs.

Materials Needed:
- one copy of the Braille alphabet (page 122) for each participant
- paper and pencils

Procedure:
1. Choose a partner.

2. Write a message to your partner in Braille. As you write, leave plenty of space between the lines. Don't forget to indicate capital letters and to use periods when they are needed.

3. Check the Braille letters you have written against the alphabet on page 122 to be certain that the dots are in the correct places.

4. When you are certain that the Braille message you have written is correct, give it to your partner.

5. Ask your partner to read your message. Then ask him or her to transcribe it in the answer space and write a reply in Braille on a separate sheet of paper for you to transcribe.

Can you read the message below?

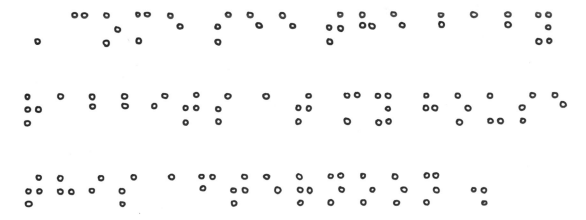

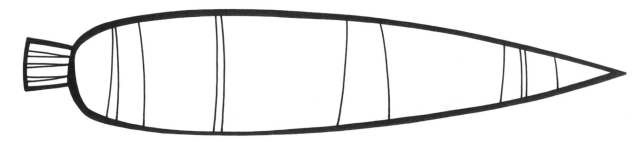

LET'S READ A STORY IN BRAILLE

Purpose: This activity gives children an opportunity to compare a Braille book to a printed book.

Materials Needed:
- 2 copies of the same book, one in Braille and one in print

Call your local school district for the name and phone number of a teacher who works with students who are visually impaired. She or he would have access to Braille textbooks and books of various reading levels or would be able to provide you with another contact person.

Procedure:

At story time, bring out both books. Announce the name of the story and share with the class both copies of the same book. The students will want to feel the book and comment about their observations.

Guest Reader:

If possible, invite a youngster with a visual impairment to visit your class and read the story. The actual demonstration by a peer is very effective in providing insight as to how people with visual impairments read. The guest reader would also be able to answer questions that the children may have.

Another guest reader might be a transcriber of Braille books.

Alphabet cards and other teaching materials are available through the American Printing House for the Blind, 1839 Frankfort Avenue, P.O. Box 6085, Louisville, KY 40206-0085; 800-572-0844.

A VISION CHECK: HOW WELL DO YOU SEE?

Directions: Tape this page to the floor and stand with your toes touching the bottom edge of the paper. Read the lines of print starting with the largest at the bottom. Stop when you come to a line of print that you can't read. DO NOT bend over while you read.

10. player
12. quiet
14. later
16. book
18. sleep
20. noise
22. class
24. vision
26. hill top
28. flowers
30. sentence
32. doorstep
34. windows
36. telephone

White Cane Safety Day, October 15 — an annual awareness day

The white cane is a symbol of the independence of the blind. It is used to promote public awareness of the blind as equal and productive citizens within the community.

SPECTACLE SPECULATION

Purpose: This activity helps children who have never worn eyeglasses or had problems with their vision to empathize with those who wear glasses (spectacles) because of a visual impairment.

Materials Needed:
- a mirror
- eyeglass frames without lenses (Obtain discarded frames from an oculist, optician, or optometrist or ask students to bring some from home.)
- squiggled glasses prepared for the activity on page 69–70.
- a copy of the book: *Spectacles* by Ellen Raskin (New York: Atheneum, 1972)
- a copy of the Snellen Eye Chart

Procedure:
1. Read the book to the class.

2. Discuss the main character's need for vision correction or glasses.

3. Make the mirror and eyeglass frames available at a learning center area.

4. Suggest that children take turns trying on frames and looking at themselves in the mirror.

5. Discuss how it feels to wear glasses. Based on their comments, encourage them to speculate about how it feels to be permanently visually impaired and to wear glasses all of the time.

6. Check the bibliotherapy list under the heading *vision* for other books to read to the class.

7. How do you know if you need glasses? Display the Snellen Eye chart and explain how it is used to test visual acuity. Do the activity How Well Do You See? on page 128, or set up the room to show the Snellen Eye Chart procedure.

8. Ask a student who has a vision problem and wears glasses to talk with the class about some of his or her experiences.

9. Arrange for the school nurse or some other qualified person to do vision screening in your classroom while students watch and ask questions.

IT'S KIND OF BLURRY

Purpose: To increase awareness of various visual impairments

Materials Needed:
- cellophane
- plastic soda can holders cut into sections to resemble eyeglass frames
- pipe cleaners
- scissors
- pencils
- various kinds of tape: opaque adhesive, masking, frosted, and transparent

Procedure:
1. Have students create a pair of eyeglass frames using the pipe cleaners as the ear pieces and the soda can holders as the lens holders.

2. Select one of the vision impairments and recreate that lens (see illustration).

3. After students have constructed a pair of glasses, challenge them to complete a school assignment while wearing their vision impairment glasses.

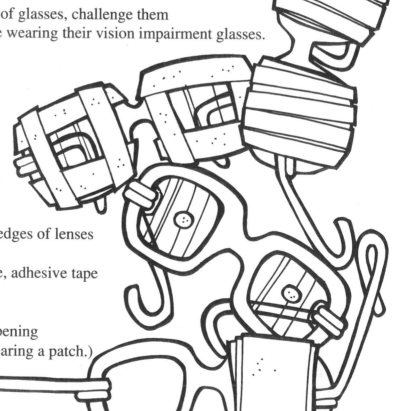

Blindness
Opaque adhesive tape over openings
Low Vision with Light Perception
Masking tape over openings
Cataracts
Cellophane lenses with small, opaque, adhesive tape circles
Tunnel Vision
Opaque adhesive tape around outside edges of lenses
Peripheral Vision
Cellophane lenses with a large, opaque, adhesive tape circle in the center of each lens
Loss of Stereo Vision
Opaque adhesive tape over one lens opening
(This also simulates the effect of wearing a patch.)

Discussion:
Encourage participants to share their newly-discovered insights about how much they rely on their sense of vision.
- What other methods or devices can be used to help a person see better?
- What should you do to protect your eyes out of doors in bright light?

AN EYE-CATCHING BOARD

Materials Needed:
- paper letters to spell "The Eyes Have It!"
- a labeled anatomical drawing of the human eye (page 119)
- drawings and photographs of a variety of eyes, including some belonging to people and some belonging to animals and insects

Procedure:
1. Put the caption at the top of the bulletin board.
2. In the center of the board, post the anatomical drawing.
3. Arrange a variety of eye pictures around the drawing.
4. Encourage students to add pictures and drawings to the display as they find them.

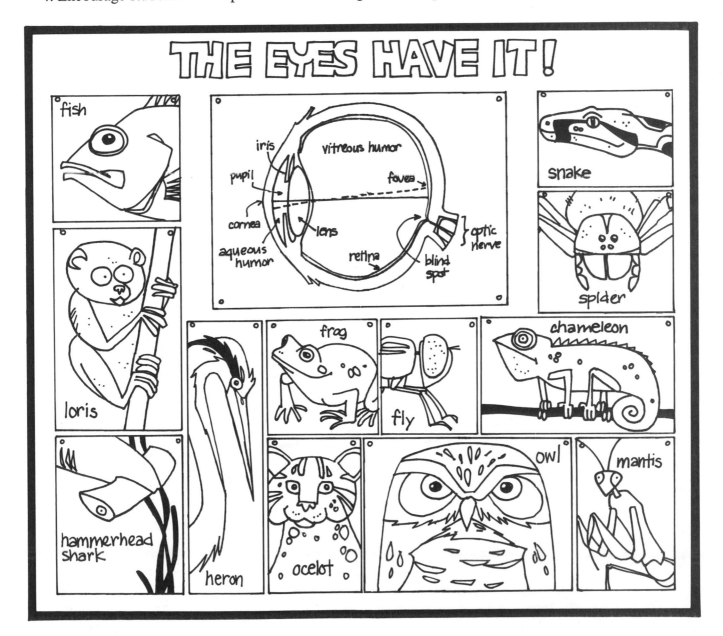

CURRICULUM-RELATED ACTIVITIES

Art:

- **Successful art repeated:**

  Choose an art experience and media that the class has enjoyed but this time ask students to wear mittens, socks, or rubber gloves on their hands while doing the activity. Encourage a group discussion on reactions to the experience and how it might feel to have trouble with fine motor control.

Language Arts

- **Creative writing assignment topics:**

  Assign a short story title that relates to physical disabilities. Examples might be: The Wild Wheelchair Ride, A Brace for Me, Spectacular Magic Spectacles, or My Two-Wheeler is a Chair.

- **Essay writing:**

  Create a list of physical disabilities and allow students to select one as a topic for a brief essay. The following information could be included: description of the disability, accommodations, safety precautions, convenience tips, the probable reactions to it, and feelings about it.

Math

- **Fast math:**

  Have the students put on thick mittens or large rubber gloves and then assign a new timed math exercise to be completed. Reactions will vary, but this math will not be boring.

Movement

- **Obstacle course maneuvers:**

  Set up a course using chairs, desks, traffic cones, tires, rocks, boxes, planks, boards, and a ramp. Borrow wheelchairs from local rental agencies, hospitals, or retirement complexes. Have students who are not physically disabled attempt to negotiate the course in chairs. Afterward, encourage them to talk about the problems they had and how they overcame them.

- **What a walk!**

  Try an outdoor relay with children walking in sacks. A variation on this activity would be to walk with your legs tied together or use borrowed crutches on a preplanned route. Make sure that each child who is simulating this disabled walk has a capable guide in case assistance is needed.

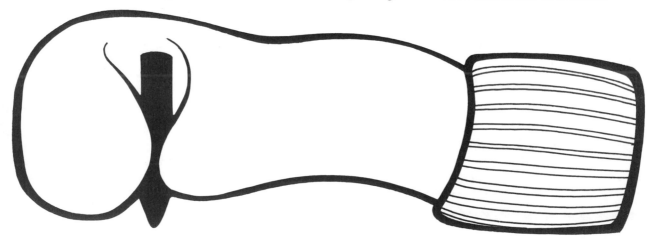

CHAPTER 6
FACTS ABOUT OTHER HEALTH CONDITIONS

INTRODUCTION

Classroom teachers are faced with many unexpected situations. In trying to meet the needs of every student, the teacher may come to the conclusion that every child is a special needs child. Frequently, a child enrolled in a regular classroom and participating in regular activities will have a medical condition that needs to be explained to classmates.

This chapter provides facts and resources on special health topics and conditions for which the classroom teacher may need basic information. In turn, teachers can use this information to guide discussion and handle questions from students. Not all conditions addressed in this chapter are specifically considered disabilities, but they are included because teachers often need basic information on these conditions.

The conditions covered are allergies, AIDS, asthma, attention deficit disorder, autism, cancer, cerebral palsy, cleft palate/craniofacial deformities, cystic fibrosis, diabetes, Down syndrome, epilepsy, heart problems, spina bifida, and skin conditions that include birthmarks, burns, and eczema.

DID YOU KNOW?

- The U.S. Department of Education has reported that it provides services to over 100,000 students with disabilities, about sixteen percent of school enrollment nationwide.
- Yearly, about seven percent, or 260,000 children, are born below the normal birth weight of five and a half pounds. (Education Commission of the States)
- Fourteen million children of all ages have been exposed to damaging levels of lead, with the most apparent damage occurring to the central nervous system. (Education Commission of the States)
- Every year approximately 35,000 babies are born to girls under the age of fifteen. (*New York Times*)
- Twenty-three percent of America's children under the age of six live in poverty. (National Center for Children in Poverty)

EDUCATIONAL IMPLICATIONS

To be effective, educational programs need to incorporate a variety of components to meet the considerable needs of individuals with severe or multiple disabilities. Programs should assess needs in four major areas: domestic, leisure/recreational, community, and vocational.

These assessments enable teachers and other professionals to identify functional objectives (objectives that will result in the learner's increased skill and independence in dealing with the routine activities of his or her life). Instruction for all students should include the expression of choice, communication skills, functional skill development, and age-appropriate social skills training.

Related services are of great importance, and the multidisciplinary approach is crucial. Appropriate people such as speech and language therapists, physical and occupational therapists, and medical specialists need to work closely with classroom teachers and parents. Because of problems with the generalization of skills, related services are best offered during the natural routine within the school and community rather than by removing a student from class for isolated therapy.

Frequently, classroom arrangements must take into consideration students' needs for medications, special diets, or special equipment. Adaptive aids and equipment enable students to increase their functional range. For example, in recent years computers have become effective communication devices for the disabled. Computerized communication equipment and specially built vocational equipment also play important roles in adapting working environments for people with serious movement limitations. Other aids include wheelchairs, typewriters, head-sticks (headgear), clamps, modified handles on cups and silverware, and communication boards.

Integration with peers who are not disabled is an important component of the educational setting. Attending the same school and participating in the same activities with the peer group is crucial to the development of social skills and friendships for people with severe disabilities.

Resources
- *Since Owen: A Parent-to-Parent Guide for the Care of the Disabled Child*, by C. Callahan. John Hopkins University Press, 1990.
- *Educating Children with Multiple Disabilities: A Transdisciplinary Approach*, Second Edition, by F. Orelove and D. Sobsey. Paul H. Brookes, 1991.
- *Healthy Young Children: A Manual for Programs*, edited by Abby Kendrick, Roxane Kaufmann, and Katherine Messenger. NAEYC, 1993.

ALLERGIES

What is an allergy? What is hay fever? Allergic rhinitis or hay fever is often experienced as a reaction in the nose to irritants or "allergens" in the environment. Common allergens that trigger hay fever are pollen, dust, dust mites, mold, animal dander, and certain foods. Symptoms may include chronic nasal stuffiness, a runny nose, coughing, wheezing, or difficulty in breathing.

What are some other common allergies?

Many people experience allergies to certain foods. One of the more common food allergies is an intolerance to milk or milk products. About three children in 100 develop this allergy. This usually appears in the first few months of life, when an infant's digestive system is still immature. Children with milk allergies need to avoid not only milk, but all dairy products made from milk.

Other common sources of allergens include citrus foods, foods containing wheat or grains; nuts; shellfish; pets, especially animals with fur or feathers; and molds, which grow both indoors and out, especially in damp climates.

What is the treatment?

Children with allergies may be on medications to treat the symptoms. Antihistamines, decongestants, and anti-asthma medications may need to be administered daily by the school nurse or a designated adult.

AIDS

As of June 1994, over 5,700 children under the age of 13 have tested HIV positive or have contracted AIDS nationwide.

What is AIDS?

AIDS stands for Acquired Immunodeficiency Syndrome. It is caused by the human immunodeficiency virus (HIV). HIV primarily affects the body by destroying its ability to fight diseases and infections.

How do children get AIDS?

Most children receive the virus from an infected mother before or during birth or while breast feeding, or they get it from blood transfusions. Children with hemophilia have been infected with the virus through the blood components in plasma.

Children won't get HIV from handshakes, coughs or sneezes, sweat or tears, or mosquitoes or other insects. They won't get the virus from being around an infected person or from swimming pools, toilet seats, phones or computers, straws, spoons, cups, food, or drinking fountains.

AIDS

What is the treatment and cure?

At this time, there is no cure. Scientists expect that finding a vaccine or a cure will take many more years of research. However, people can help prevent the spread of HIV infection by learning the facts about HIV and AIDS and protecting themselves and others. Treatment involves a variety of drugs, with more being tried all the time. Eating a nutritious diet and avoiding infections are also important for children with AIDS.

References

- *AIDS, Department of Health and Human Services*: a pamphlet that answers questions frequently asked about AIDS. It covers causes, symptoms, transmission, treatment, and prevention.

- Centers for Disease Control, Office of Public Affairs, 1600 Clifton Road NE, Building 1, Room 2167, Atlanta, GA 30333.

- AIDS hotline: 1-800-342-2437.

Organizations for Children Concerned about AIDS

- Positively Pediatrics and Adolescents: provides education and support services for family members and friends of HIV-positive children. Speakers and community materials are also available. P.O. Box 4512, Queensbury, NY 12804; 518-798-8940.

- AIDS Hotline for Kids: 415-435-5022.

Classroom Activity

The AIDS Traveling Quilt Exhibit is a memorial that circulates throughout the United States in memory of those individuals who have died from AIDS. You can find out when the quilt exhibit will be in your area by contacting: Names Project Foundation, 310 Townsend, Suite 310, San Francisco, CA 94107; 415-882-5500.

Students can construct their own quilt honoring people with special needs. Cover a bulletin board with brown wrapping paper and then section the board with black yarn. Each student should be given the same size paper or fabric square to design with crayons, paint, or other art materials. The squares can be laced together with yarn or stapled to the board.

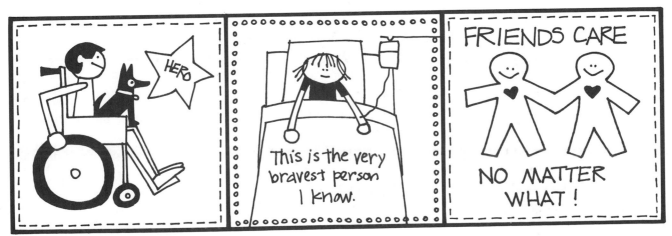

ASTHMA

Asthma is the leading cause of chronic illness in children. It is estimated to occur in five to ten percent of children during their developmental years. Before puberty, twice as many boys as girls have asthma, but in adults the incidence is about equal.

What is asthma?

Asthma is a chronic condition in which breathing becomes difficult because of mucus in the air sacs of the lungs and tightening of the bronchial tubes. Symptoms of asthma include shortness of breath, coughing, and wheezing (whistling sounds during breathing).

What is an asthma attack?

An asthma attack is characterized by periodic, sudden episodes of coughing, wheezing, and shortness of breath. During an asthma attack, cells in the lungs release histamine and other chemicals that cause the bronchial tubes to constrict and the air sacs to fill with mucus.

What causes an asthma attack?

Many things can trigger an asthma attack. In children under five, an attack most commonly occurs if a viral respiratory infection inflames the lining of the bronchial tubes and stimulates the muscles surrounding them to constrict. Other common triggers of asthma attacks include air pollutants, such as cigarette smoke or paint fumes, stress and emotional upsets, respiratory infections, certain medications, exercise, or inhaling cold air. Allergens such as pollens, mold spores, or animal danders can also provoke an attack.

Emergency Care

Emergency medical services should be called if a child has severe trouble breathing and seems to be getting worse — especially if breathing is rapid and accompanied by a pulling in of the chest upon inhaling and a forceful grunting upon exhaling. Blue fingertips; darkened skin; or agitated, lethargic, or confused behavior are other serious signs that medical help should be obtained.

Treatment

Physicians generally advise asthma patients to avoid known triggers such as house dust, pet dander, tobacco smoke, and strong odors, as well as known allergens such as pollen, mold spores, and foods. They often recommend humidified air in cold, dry weather. The short-term use of bronchodilator aerosols is effective, but physicians caution that it is important to follow dosage recommendations carefully. Acute attacks may be relieved by a number of drugs such as epinephrine, an adrenal hormone that helps relax and expand the bronchial tubes.

Classroom Activities:

1. Read one of the bibliotherapy books and lead a class discussion.
2. Teach or review basic health issues such as hand washing and good nutrition.
3. Ask a nurse-educator or other health professional to visit and talk about asthma and allergies, using a chest and lung poster.
4. Create an asthma and allergy hospital in your dramatic play lessons. Stock the play corner with lab coats, surgical gloves, x-rays, folders for medical records, disposable masks and mouthpieces, stethoscopes, ambulance drivers' hats, etc.
5. Ask a parent familiar with a nebulizer to bring it in and demonstrate to the class what it does for a child with asthma.
6. Ask an older student to visit the class and talk about his or her difficulties and ways to cope with asthma or allergies.

ATTENTION DEFICIT DISORDER

No firm statistics are kept on attention deficit disorder, but it is estimated that between three and five percent of all children are affected.

What is attention deficit disorder?

Attention Deficit Disorder (ADD), also called Attention Deficit Hyperactivity Disorder (ADHD), is a developmental disability characterized by three predominant features: inattention, impulsiveness, and, in many but not all cases, restlessness or hyperactivity. The disorder is most prevalent in children and is generally thought of as a childhood disorder. Recent studies show that ADD can and does continue throughout the adult years. Current estimates suggest that approximately 50 to 65 percent of children with ADD will have symptoms of the disorder as adolescents and adults.

What causes ADD?

Scientists and medical experts do not know precisely what causes ADD. Evidence suggests that the disorder is genetically transmitted in many cases and is caused by a chemical imbalance. ADD appears to be a neurologically-based medical problem and is not caused by poor parenting or diet.

What are the characteristics of ADD?

The signs of ADD are inattention, impulsiveness, hyperactivity, poor motor control, disorganization, and social skill deficits. From time to time, all children can display inattention and impulsiveness and can exhibit high energy levels. With the ADD child, these behaviors are the rule, not the exception. Keep in mind that some degree of difficulty exists with every child.

What are the medical implications?

A thorough medical work-up done by a specialist is the first step in diagnosis. Effective treatment of ADD generally requires the following: education about the disorder, training in the use of behavior management, medication when indicated, and an appropriate educational program.

Attention Deficit Disorder

What are the educational implications?

Here are some guidelines for working with the ADD student:

- The classroom environment needs to be structured and predictable, with rules, schedules, and assignments posted and clearly spelled out.
- The best seating for the ADD child is close to the teacher, away from distractions.
- Directions should be clear and simple and should be given a few at a time.
- The curriculum will need to be modified in accordance with the child's organizational skills and his or her ability to pay attention and concentrate.
- All tasks need to be monitored.
- Behavior management is critical. Behavior charts, used in combination with other educational interventions, often produce positive results.

Self-esteem is vital!

Most undiagnosed and untreated children with ADD suffer from low self-esteem. Many also show signs of being mildly depressed. These feelings stem from the child's sense of personal failure. For the child with ADD, the world is often an unkind place. (See The Cycle of Success in Chapter 1.)

References

- *The ADD Hyperactivity Workbook for Parents, Teachers, and Kids*, by H. C. Parker. Impact Publications, 1988.
- *ADHD/Hyperactivity: A Consumer's Guide*, by M. Gordon. GSI Publications, 1990.
- *Maybe You Know My Kid: A Parent's Guide to Identifying, Understanding, and Helping Your Child with ADHA*, by M. C. Fowler. Birch Lane Press, 1990.

Classroom Activities

1. Ask children to keep daily journals in which they write about or draw a picture of one event that occurred during the day that made them feel good about themselves. Include a teacher's page and a parent's page in each journal where adults can record words of encouragement to the child.

2. Use a highlighter pen to emphasize exemplary portions of students' written work. Recommend that each child in the class start a "PRIDE" folder to store papers and anecdotal records of classroom events that affirm the child's academic and social accomplishments. Encourage students to share their folders with other school personnel and their parents.

AUTISM*

Autism occurs approximately ten to fifteen times in 10,000 births. This disorder is four times more common in boys than in girls.

What is autism?

Autism is a developmental disability significantly affecting verbal and nonverbal communication and social interaction. It is generally evident before the age of three. This disorder affects a child's ability to communicate, understand language, play, and relate to others. The cause is unknown. Currently, researchers are investigating areas such as neurological damage and biochemical imbalance in the brain. Autism is not caused by psychological factors.

How do autistic children behave?

Children with autism vary greatly in ability, intelligence, and behavior. Some do not speak; others have limited language that often includes repeated phrases or conversations. Those with more advanced language skills tend to stick to a few topics and have difficulty with abstract concepts. Repetitive play skills, a limited range of interests, and impaired social skills are common. Unusual responses to sensory information — for example, loud noises, lights, or certain textures of food or fabrics — are also common.

What are the educational implications?

Educational programs focus on improving communication and social, academic, behavioral, and daily living skills. Behavior and communication problems that interfere with learning require the assistance of a knowledgeable professional trained in autism-specific teaching strategies.

The classroom environment should be structured so that the program is consistent and predictable. Students with autism learn better and are less confused when information is presented visually as well as verbally. Interaction with nondisabled peers is also important, for these students provide models of appropriate language and social and behavioral skills. To overcome frequent problems in the generalization of skills learned at school, it is important to develop programs with parents so that learning activities, experiences, and approaches can be carried over into the home and community environment.

References
- *Children with Autism: A Parent's Guide*, by M. D. Powers, editor. Woodbine House, 1989.
- *Handbook of Autism and Pervasive Developmental Disorders*, by D. J. Cohen and A. M. Donnellan. V. H. Winston & Sons, 1987.
- *A Parent's Guide to Autism: Answers to the Most Common Questions*, by C. A. Hart. Simon & Schuster, 1993.

* Information adapted with permission from brochures from the National Information Center for Children and Youth with Disabilities, 1-800-695-0285.

CANCER/LEUKEMIA

No nationwide cancer registry exists, so there is no way of knowing exactly how many new cases of cancer are diagnosed each year. Cancer occurs throughout the world; no country and no population is free of it, not even children.

What is cancer?

Cancer is actually a group of diseases, each with its own name, treatment, and chances for control or cure. Cancer occurs when a particular cell or group of cells begins to multiply and grow uncontrollably, crowding out the normal cells. Cancer may take the form of leukemia, which develops from the white blood cells, or solid tumors that can be found in any part of the body.

What are the medical implications?

Children with cancer may be on medication and may have periodic hospital visits. A child in school may be having chemotherapy or radiation treatments. Side effects of the medications and treatments vary widely. Each drug has the potential to produce its own side effects. The child's parents can tell school personnel which side effects their child is most likely to experience. Some are nausea and vomiting, allergic reactions (hives, rash, shortness of breath, or swelling of eyelids, hands, or feet), hair loss, mouth sores and ulcers, jaundice (yellow tint to the skin and eyes due to liver problems), and a mental or nervous system change causing lethargy and fatigue or lack of coordination. A child's physical appearance may also change.

What are the educational implications?

Continuing with school is vital for the school-age child. School is the major activity of children, and continuing to attend school reinforces the child's sense of well-being. Consistent school attendance prevents the child from falling behind in academic areas and in the emotional-social development that comes from participating in school and school activities. When a hospital stay is necessary, either a hospital school program can be instituted or a home tutor can be arranged through the school system. It is important that all school personnel have the correct information about each child and the type of cancer and special considerations indicated.

Children with cancer fear rejection from peers and will need help dealing with this issue. Classroom teachers need to be aware of a child's fears. They must remember that classmates will have questions about the child's cancer and any changes in appearance. It is important to help children anticipate these questions and answer them.

Discipline is a delicate issue at school and at home. Although it is true that for many of these young people the future is uncertain and some will die, discipline is an important part of seeing that the quality of life is maintained. Parents or teachers should be aware of the temptation to overprotect the child.

References
- American Cancer Society, 1-800-ACS-2345, and the National Cancer Institute provide many publications for parents and teachers.
- *A Resource Guide for Parents of Children with Cancer*, published by the American Cancer Society, is comprehensive.

CEREBRAL PALSY

Each year about 5,000 babies are born with cerebral palsy or acquire it early in life. Overall, about 500,000 persons in the United States have cerebral palsy. Teenagers and young adults comprise about one-third of that number. Cerebral palsy is one of the most widespread lifetime disabilities in the nation.

What is cerebral palsy?

Cerebral palsy is a term used to describe a variety of conditions characterized by lack of muscle control. Symptoms vary greatly among individuals, and an individual may exhibit one or more symptoms to varying degrees. Symptoms include disturbance in gait or mobility; lack of balance; shaking or involuntary movements; stiffness; limpness; loss of manual dexterity; seizures; mental retardation; and problems with vision, hearing, and speech.

What causes cerebral palsy?

Cerebral palsy is caused by damage to the part of the brain that controls and coordinates muscular action. Most often it occurs before or during delivery or immediately after birth because the supply of oxygen to the fetal or newborn brain is interrupted. Premature birth and low birth weight is associated with an increased risk of cerebral palsy. A baby can also get cerebral palsy from severe jaundice after birth or can develop it later in infancy from a brain injury or an illness affecting the brain.

Can it be prevented?

Cerebral palsy can often be prevented by ensuring that pregnant women obtain good prenatal care and avoid exposure to medications and x-rays unless monitored by a physician. After birth, a baby can be protected from brain damage by careful handling, proper care, and vaccination against childhood diseases.

How and when is it detected?

Infants with cerebral palsy may have difficulty sucking, or have floppy or tight muscles. Often the first sign of trouble is slow development of the infant's muscular control and coordination. Routine physical examinations and early intervention and therapy during the infant and toddler years are important.

What is the treatment and cure?

Depending on the type of cerebral palsy, early intervention programs can be effective. Children with cerebral palsy participate in many kinds of therapy: physical, occupational, speech, and hearing. In some cases, braces are worn to reinforce a muscle group. Medication may help reduce muscle tension and limit other problems that involve nerve damage. Bioengineering technology is creating many new devices to increase the mobility of persons with cerebral palsy and to improve their ability to communicate.

Classroom Activities

1. Invite a health professional to speak to the class about cerebral palsy.

2. Locate a video about cerebral palsy. Check with medical clinics, teaching colleges, the local health department, or your local United Cerebral Palsy affiliate.

3. Invite a child with cerebral palsy to visit the class and talk about his or her disability.

4. Have a class discussion about how it may feel to have some of the symptoms of cerebral palsy.

CLEFT PALATE/CRANIOFACIAL DEFORMITIES

What is a craniofacial deformity?

A craniofacial deformity is a general term for any abnormality of the face and/or head. These deformities can be congenital (occurring at birth, such as cleft lip/palate) or acquired (occurring due to trauma or disase such as an accident or cancer). Cleft lip and palate are the most common of the congenital deformities.

What is a cleft lip and/or palate?

Cleft lip and/or palate is the fourth most frequent birth defect in the United States, occurring in one out of every 700 births. More than 5,000 children are affected each year. A cleft lip is a separation of the two sides of the upper lip. The separation may also include the gum and nose. A cleft palate is an opening in the roof of the mouth in which the two sides of the palate did not fuse or join together as the unborn baby was developing. A cleft lip is visible while a cleft palate is not. Children with cleft palate often have speech and hearing difficulties. Teachers should be sensitive to their special needs.

Is surgery necessary?

Most children will require several surgical treatments to achieve a more normal appearance and function.

What kind of reaction can you expect?

Most adults don't want to offend someone who looks "different" and will hurry their own children away to avoid embarrassment. Instead, allow children and their parents time to do some "sustained staring." Be prepared to talk naturally with and about the affected child. Adjustment time varies. Most young children get used to differences in appearance fairly quickly. Older children may need more help with understanding and accepting these differences.

Classroom Activities

- Invite the parents to visit the classroom and tell "the story about their special child." These parents will have had practice with all kinds of situations.

- The movie "Mask" features a youngster with a craniofacial deformity. Show part of the movie to the class to generate discussion. Watch the June newspapers for information on the annual Cher's Family Retreat Weekend. The weekend includes informational sessions, local attractions, and plenty of time for adults to interact and kids to play.

- Set up a tabletop manipulative activity. Cut large photos of faces from magazines. Laminate the pictures and cut the faces in halves or thirds. Cut one set of pictures horizontally and another set vertically. Use these sets for matching games during free time. A set of class photographs also can be used in this fashion. This activity stimulates discussion of facial features, similarities, and differences.

- Contact the Cleft Palate Foundation. They will send an information packet to help kids learn more about cleft lip/palate. Their toll-free number is 800-24-CLEFT.

- About Face, an international support organization for individuals and families affected by craniofacial conditions, has a school program. If there is a chapter in your community, invite a representative to your class to make a presentation.

CYSTIC FIBROSIS

Cystic fibrosis occurs in about one of every 2,000 Caucasian babies and in about one of every 17,000 African-American babies. Cystic fibrosis is rare in Asians and Native Americans. About 2,000 babies in the United States are born with cystic fibrosis every year. The disease occurs equally in males and females.

What is cystic fibrosis?

Cystic fibrosis (usually called CF) is an inherited disease that causes certain glands in the body to fail to function normally. Cystic fibrosis is not contagious. The exocrine glands usually produce thin, slippery secretions that include sweat, mucus, tears, saliva, and digestive juices. These secretions are carried through ducts or small tubes to the outside surface of the body. In cystic fibrosis, the mucus-producing exocrine glands produce thick, sticky secretions that plug the ducts leading to the outside surface of the body. These plugs most often occur in the lungs and intestines and can interfere with vital body functions like breathing or digestion.

What are the medical implications?

Cystic fibrosis is a disease with many disguises. The exact symptoms and the severity of symptoms can vary greatly from person to person. Some of the characteristics are recurrent wheezing, a persistent cough and excessively thick mucus, recurrent pneumonia, failure to gain weight despite a good appetite, abnormal bowel movements, salty tasting skin, nasal polyps, and clubbing (enlargement of the fingertips and toes). Children with cystic fibrosis may be on daily enzyme supplements or medications, chest physical therapy, or in personalized exercise programs. The latest research in cystic fibrosis is exploring gene therapy.

What are the educational implications?

Cystic fibrosis is a serious chronic illness. Like any other chronic illness, it can cause social, emotional, and psychological problems. Adults need to observe the child with cystic fibrosis and take cues from the child about what questions to ask. Teachers and parents need to treat the child with respect and avoid being overly protective. School outbreaks of viral infections can directly affect the health of a child with cystic fibrosis. Physical restrictions may need to be placed on a child with cystic fibrosis.

References
- *An Introduction to Cystic Fibrosis for Patients and Families*, by James C. Cunningham and Lynn M. Taussig. Publication No. N855B-3/93, available from the Cystic Fibrosis Foundation.

Classroom Activity

Have students do research to learn five facts about cystic fibrosis. Working in pairs or small groups, students can write a short story in which the main character is a child with cystic fibrosis. Have them incorporate what they learned during their research.

DIABETES

Approximately 13 million Americans suffer from diabetes. Worldwide, it is estimated that there are between 100 and 150 million people with diabetes.

What is Diabetes or Diabetes Mellitus?

Diabetes Mellitus is a chronic metabolic disorder that adversely affects the body's ability to manufacture and utilize insulin. Insulin is a hormone necessary for the conversion of food into energy. There are two major types of diabetes: Type 1, also known as juvenile diabetes, and Type II, or maturity-onset diabetes. Juvenile diabetes can appear at any age, though it is most commonly diagnosed from infancy to the late thirties. Maturity-onset diabetes usually begins in the middle or later years. Diabetes is not contagious.

What is the treatment and cure?

There is no cure yet, but diabetes can be successfully controlled. The three elements of diabetes "control" are food, exercise, and insulin. Diabetes control is a constant balancing of these three factors. Food intake makes the glucose (sugar) level rise; exercise and insulin make the glucose level fall. People with juvenile diabetes must take daily insulin injections to stay alive. They also monitor their blood sugar levels several times a day using a special machine. For maturity-onset diabetes, oral medication or insulin may be taken, and diet and weight control can help.

What are the medical considerations?

The first step for the classroom teacher is to talk with the parents of the child with diabetes. Taking food and medications on time is critical. Physical activity, fatigue, excitement, anxiety, and illness can upset the balance of sugar and insulin in the child's system and a blood sugar imbalance may result. This imbalance is sometimes referred to as hypoglycemia (low blood sugar) or hyperglycemia (high blood sugar). Each child reacts differently to a sugar imbalance and the child's parents can give teachers specific guidelines about their child.

What are the symptoms of a blood sugar imbalance?

The rapidly appearing symptoms of a low blood sugar (hypoglycemia) may include crying, confusion, irritability, paleness, perspiring, shakiness, drowsiness, inattention, headaches, nausea, hunger, or feeling weak. Symptoms of a high blood sugar (hyperglycemia) may include excessive thirst and frequent urination.

Tips on what to do during and after a low blood sugar

Treatment priority is to get sugary food into the child fast! Fruit juice, candy, non-diet soda, or glucose tablets are suggested. If necessary, liquid sugar, jam, or honey can be rubbed on the inside of the child's cheek with a finger. Once the reaction subsides, the child should eat to prevent a recurrence. Milk, bread, or cheese and crackers are advised. When any child is suspected of having a low blood sugar, it is important that the child be under direct adult supervision. Get emergency help if the child is unconscious or unable to swallow.

What are the educational implications?

If you are supervising a child with diabetes, you should be aware that children with diabetes can lead a normal school life. They have the same need for guidance, support, and understanding as other children.

DIABETES

General Guidelines for a Child With Diabetes

Because diet is such a critical factor for a youngster with diabetes, the following concerns are important. Teachers need to ask the child's parents about specific guidelines for their child.

- Observe the child's behavior before meals and snacks. Try not to assign strenuous physical exercise just before a meal when the child's blood sugar level may be dropping.

- Recess breaks are an inconspicuous snack time for youngsters with diabetes who need mid-morning and/or afternoon snacks; however, if a child with diabetes needs to eat during class time, the child should be made to feel comfortable about it. Teachers need to be aware of time schedules if a child needs to inject insulin or monitor blood sugar levels.

- Keep fast sugar readily available (orange juice, non-diet soda, candy, or sugar itself). Make sure all aides, specialists, or substitutes know how to access the classroom sugar supply.

- Make sure all school personnel are aware and informed, including substitute teachers.

- Keep parent-approved treats in the classroom for the child with diabetes. Birthday celebrations, Halloween, and Valentine's Day are difficult events for any child who must control food or sugar intake. Generally acceptable snacks for the child with diabetes are popcorn, sugar-free popsicles, peanuts, fresh vegetables, or cheese.

- Be sure to take snacks and emergency sugar sources on field trips.

- Work with the child's parents to include insulin, syringes, etc. in the school's disaster or emergency supplies.

- Illness can be a problem for someone with diabetes. Find out from the child's parents what procedures you should follow in the event of fever or vomiting that develops at school.

References
- Juvenile Diabetes Foundation, 800-JDF-CURE, has many excellent references and a video available.

DIABETES

Classroom Activities

- Invite the child with diabetes to speak to the class and answer questions.

- Have students do research to find out more about the pancreas and the function it serves in the body.

- Following a class discussion on sugar and its effects on diet, the class could choose from the following activities:

  - read ingredient labels to determine the contents of a food product.

  - identify foods in which sugar is the first or second ingredient. Learn the names of other sweeteners—high fructose corn syrup, dextrose, sucrose, honey, molasses, etc.—and find them in the ingredient lists as well.

  - design a list of healthy snacks vs. empty calorie snacks.

DOWN SYNDROME*

Approximately 4,000 children with Down syndrome are born in the United States each year; that's about one in every 800 to 1,000 live births. Although women of any age may have a child with Down syndrome, the incidence is higher for women over the age of thirty-five.

What is Down syndrome?

Down syndrome is the most common and readily identifiable chromosomal condition associated with developmental impairment. It is caused by a chromosomal abnormality. Cell development occurs with forty-seven instead of the usual forty-six chromosomes.

How does Down syndrome affect a child's appearance?

Youngsters with Down syndrome are usually smaller than their nondisabled peers, and their physical as well as intellectual development is slower. More than fifty clinical characteristics have been identified with the syndrome, but it's rare to find all or even most of them in one person. Some common characteristics are

- slanting eyes with folds of skin at the inner corners (called epicanthal folds)

- hyperflexibility (excessive ability to extend the joints)

- short, broad hands with a single crease across the palm of one or both hands

- broad feet with short toes; a flat bridge on the nose; short, low-set ears; a short neck, and a small head

* Information adapted with permission from publications of the National Information Center for Children and Youth with Disabilities, 1-800-695-0285.

DOWN SYNDROME

What are the educational implications?

Research has shown that stimulation during early developmental stages improves the child's chances of developing to his or her fullest potential. Continuing education, positive public attitudes, and a stimulating home environment have also been found to promote the child's overall development. The level of mental impairment, behavior, and developmental progress in individuals with this syndrome varies widely. Due to this fact, it is impossible to predict future achievements for children with Down syndrome.

Because of the range of ability in children with Down syndrome, it is important for families and members of the school's educational team to place few limitations on potential capabilities. It may be effective to emphasize concrete concepts rather than abstract ideas. Teaching tasks in a step-by-step manner with frequent reinforcement and consistent feedback has proven successful. Independent living centers, group-shared and supervised apartments, and support services in the community are important resources for persons with Down syndrome.

References

• *Keys to Parenting a Child with Down Syndrome*, by M. T. Brill. Barrons, 1993.

• *A Parent's Guide to Down Syndrome: Toward a Brighter Future*, by S. M. Pueschel, editor. Paul H. Brookes, 1990.

• *Babies with Down Syndrome: A New Parent's Guide*, by K. Stray-Gundersen. Woodbine House, 1986.

EPILEPSY

One out of every one hundred children has seizures. In any school, the chances are good that there will be a child who has a seizure disability.

What is a seizure?

A seizure is an electrical disturbance in the brain that causes a child's body to move and jerk suddenly. People with epilepsy can't control their movements during a seizure. Sometimes they won't know what is happening when a seizure occurs and may lose awareness of where they are and what they are doing.

What is epilepsy?

Epilepsy is a disorder of the central nervous system that causes a person to have repeated seizures. These seizures can happen any time during the day or night. Seizures are not always caused by epilepsy, but a person who has more than one seizure, even if the seizures happen at different times of the day, is said to have epilepsy.

What causes epilepsy and can it be prevented?

Doctors are not always sure what causes epilepsy. Sometimes it is inherited. Other times it is caused by a head injury that affects the brain. The best way to prevent head injuries is to wear a helmet. Helmets should be worn for all sports where head injuries can occur, such as football, hockey, skate boarding, and in-line skating.

What are the medical considerations?

Most children with epilepsy take medication. Teachers can help by reminding the child to take medicine on schedule. Explaining the seizure process to the students is also important.

Activities for the Classroom

- Read *Lee, the Rabbit with Epilepsy* or an appropriate book from the bibliotherapy list. Discuss the book with the class and ask questions. Summarize facts about seizures.

- Invite an older child who has seizures to be a guest speaker in the class. Allow children to ask all the questions they have. Be sure they understand that epilepsy is a condition, not a contagious disease. Children with different seizure types may be invited to participate.

- Use the Time-Line Activity and Game on pages 152-153 to help children become familiar with the sequence of events in a seizure.

Resources

- *Seizures and Epilepsy in Childhood: A Guide for Parents*, by J. M. Freeman and E. Pillas. Johns Hopkins University Press, 1993.

- *Issues and Answers: A Guide for Parents of Teens and Young Adults with Epilepsy*, by Eileen Kobrin. Epilepsy Foundation of America, 1991.

SEIZURE TIME-LINE ACTIVITY

Children observing an epileptic seizure will be less frightened if they are aware that epileptic behavior follows a predictable pattern, or sequence, and they know what to expect. This time line is a health and safety learning activity.

What You Do
1. Duplicate the instruction card on this page and the time-line cards on page 153. Make several copies so that more than one child can play the game at a time.
2. Cut out the instruction cards. To make them more durable, glue them to pieces of tag board.
3. Cut the time-line cards apart. Glue them to pieces of tag board or to plain 3 x 5 index cards.
4. For self-checking, number the cards in the correct order on the back.
5. To keep time-line card sets separate, use a different color to number each six-card set.
6. Laminate the cards or cover them with clear, adhesive-backed paper.

With Your Class
- Discuss the facts about epilepsy. Be sure your students understand that epilepsy is a condition, not a contagious disease.
- Describe the behavior sequence that characterizes most seizures. Explain to the children that this is the safety procedure to follow if a class member or friend has a seizure.
- Make sets of one instruction card and six time-line cards available at a learning center.
- Encourage students to use the cards during their free time to review what was discussed in class about the time line of events during a seizure.

How to Play the Seizure Time-Line Game
1. Spread out all six time-line cards.
2. Read the words and look at the pictures.
3. Recall the seizure time line discussed in class.
4. Arrange the cards in the order in which you expect the pictured events to happen.
5. Check your order by looking at the numbers on the backs of the cards.

SEIZURE TIME-LINE GAME

When a person has epilepsy, some of the cells in the person's brain act up, causing a loss of control for a short time.

The person with epilepsy may wander around, may stop and stare, or may fall down.

People nearby should clear the area of anything that might injure the person if he or she falls.

The person with epilepsy goes into convulsions and may shiver, shake, make strange noises, roll his or her eyes, foam at the mouth, wet his or her clothes, or do other unusual things. The person cannot hear or speak and does not realize what is happening. The person with epilepsy may stare and not be able to talk clearly until the seizure is over.

The person with epilepsy may feel tired and/or confused after a seizure and may want to rest. The person does not remember what happened.

The person who had the seizure will behave normally when he or she wakes up.

HEART CONDITIONS

Most heart problems in children are present at birth. These congenital defects begin in the early part of pregnancy when the heart is forming. Heart disease may also occur in children who have had rheumatic fever or an unusual complication of strep throat.

How are heart problems caused?

The heart is a muscle that pumps blood throughout the body. It is divided into four hollow sections called chambers. Blood goes from the heart to the lungs, picks up oxygen, then returns to the heart where it is pumped out to the body. As the oxygen in the blood is used up, the blood returns to the heart and the process begins again. Children with heart problems may have scarred valves that do not properly control the flow of blood between the chambers, or other factors may affect the heart's ability to function effectively.

Do children with heart problems look different from regular children?

These children may have difficulty breathing and have a bluish tint to their skin, slow or abnormal growth, or unusual weight gain. They may tire easily and feel weak.

What are the medical implications?

Children with heart problems not fully corrected by surgery or children recovering from surgery may require modifications in their daily program because their stamina and endurance do not match that of their peer group. Medication may have to be administered on a regular basis. If there is an outbreak of strep throat, school personnel must be sure to notify the parents of a child who has had rheumatic fever so the parents can take precautions.

What are the educational implications?

Modifications in the daily schedule of a child with a heart condition may include shorter periods of active play, additional rest periods or longer naps, more frequent and smaller meals, and the administration of regular medications. It is important for school personnel to obtain correct descriptions from parents and doctors of the types and amounts of activities in which these children can participate. Restrictions on activity are not usually needed because children generally pace themselves. Be prepared to explain to other students the reason for the child's limited activity and to provide opportunities for that child to excel in nonphysical areas.

Programs for the Classroom

- *Heart Treasure Chest* and *Getting to Know Your Heart* are comprehensive curriculum programs aimed at preschool through the middle grades. These programs are designed to develop positive heart health habits related to diet, physical activity, and rest. Contact your local American Heart Association for details, 1-800-AHA-USA1.

SKIN: BIRTHMARKS, BURNS, AND ECZEMA

One in every 100 children is born with a visible birthmark, usually on the head, neck, or limbs. Some are light in color, while others are dark red. Other skin marks occur as a result of accidents or allergies. Some skin conditions are inherited from parents.

What is a birthmark?

Most birthmarks are formed during pregnancy, when a certain skin area develops an abnormal blood supply. Some marks will fade as a child gets older. In other cases, cosmetic laser surgery is performed.

What is a burn?

Burns can occur at any time. When permanent damage is caused to the skin cells, the skin will remain disfigured even after healing. Most children can relate to a burn since they will have experienced touching a hot stove or getting a sunburn. Safety procedures for burns and fires, including "Stop, Drop, and Roll," need to be covered with all youngsters.

What is eczema?

Eczema is a general term used to describe a number of different skin conditions. It usually appears as reddened skin that becomes moist and oozing, occasionally resulting in small, fluid-filled bumps. When eczema becomes chronic and persists for a long time, the skin tends to thicken, dry out, and become scaly with coarse lines. Children with this type of skin condition usually have discolored skin in the bends of the elbows, behind the knees, on hands, and on the backs of wrists and ankles. Other children notice the condition because it can be itchy and the skin may flake and peel. Most children with severe eczema will be on topical medication and will need to keep their skin as dry as possible.

Activities for the Classroom

- Teach a human body unit. Discuss with children the largest organ of the body, the skin, and identify ways to keep skin healthy. Sunscreen protection is vital.

- A dermatologist or guest speaker from a burn center can provide additional information that will assist children in understanding the skin conditions discussed here.

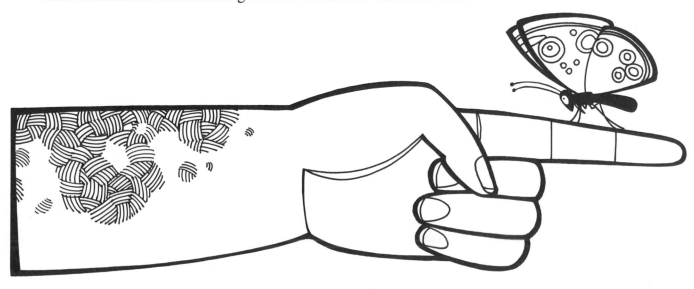

SPINA BIFIDA*

Approximately forty percent of all Americans may have a mild form of spina bifida occulta, but because they experience few or no symptoms, most never know they have it. One out of every 1,000 infants born will have spina bifida.

What is spina bifida?

Spina bifida means cleft spine, or an incomplete closure in the spinal column. There are three types of spina bifida that describe the condition in mild to severe forms: spina bifida occulta, meningocele, and myelomeningocele.

What are the medical considerations?

Many children with myelomeningocele, the most severe form of spina bifida, need training to learn to manage their bowel and bladder functions. Some require catheterization, the insertion of a tube to permit the passage of urine.

What are the educational implications?

Infants born with spina bifida usually have surgery within the first 48 hours of life to drain spinal fluid and protect against hydrocephalus. Often, these children will have a series of operations throughout childhood. In some cases, children with spina bifida who also have a history of hydrocephalus will experience learning problems. They may have difficulty paying attention, expressing or understanding language, and mastering reading and math. Early intervention with children who experience learning problems can help considerably to prepare them for school.

Can these children be mainstreamed?

A child with spina bifida sometimes requires changes in school equipment, structural accessibility, or the curriculum. Children with severe myelomeningocele need to learn mobility skills and often require the aid of crutches, braces, or wheelchairs. It is important that parents and all members of the school team understand the child's physical capabilities and limitations. Physical disabilities like spina bifida can have profound effects on a child's emotional and social development. To promote personal growth, families and teachers should encourage children, within the limits of safety and health, to be independent and to participate in activities with their nondisabled classmates.

References
- *A Parent's Guide to Spina Bifida*, by B. A. Bloom and E. S. Seljeskog. University of Minnesota Press, 1988.
- *Spina Bifida: Hope Through Research*, by the National Institute of Neurological and Communicative Disorders and Stroke. Spina Bifida Association of America, 1986.
- *Children with Spina Bifida: Early Intervention and Preschool Programming*, by G. Williamson. Brooks Publishing, 1987.

Classroom Activity

Invite a doctor who specializes in spinal cord injuries to come and talk to the class about care of the spine. If there is a chiropractic association in your area, a representative may be willing to visit your class and do a spinal check on the entire class. He or she can also discuss the importance of proper posture.

* Information adapted with permission from brochures from the National Information Center for Children and Youth with Disabilities, 1-800-695-0285.

CHAPTER 7
BIBLIOTHERAPY

INTRODUCTION

At times, every teacher and parent wishes to share insights with children but is unable to find the "right" words. Well-written children's books provide an opening for a discussion of sensitive topics and issues.

The books listed in this chapter are just the beginning of a resource list for teachers and parents of young children. New books are being published monthly. Ask your local children's librarian to notify you when a new book on the topic of disabilities appears on the shelves. Lists are included for the following conditions:

AIDS
Allergies/Asthma
Alzheimer's/Memory Loss
Appearance and Size
Cancer
Cerebral Palsy
Cystic Fibrosis
Death and Dying
Diabetes
Down Syndrome/Mental Disabilities
Epilepsy
Hearing and Signing
Learning Disabilities
Leukemia (see Cancer)
Miscellaneous:
    Dyslexia, Emotional Distress, Left-Handedness, Multiple
    Disabilities, and Multiple Sclerosis
Physical/Orthopedic Impairments
Vision
Wheelchair Use

WHAT IS BIBLIOTHERAPY?

Bibliotherapy is a more recent term for the old practice of using books to help children solve personal problems and satisfy their basic needs as they grow and mature. Ancient Greek libraries were known to have borne such descriptions as "the healing place of the soul" and the "medicine chest for the soul." Interpreted in its broadest sense, bibliotherapy is based on the belief that through empathy with characters met in books, a reader is better able to understand himself or herself and apply critical thinking skills to personal situations.

A belief in the value of bibliotherapy is a belief that quality literature has the power to change behavior, to improve attitudes, and to aid in self-awareness and understanding. A book may be considered suitable for bibliotherapy if it tells a story, yet has the power to help a reader.

Teaching Strategies and Goals

Develop strategies and use exercises and activities that help children and adults do the following:

- Learn more about the psychology and physiology of human behavior and special needs children.
- Learn what it means to "know thyself."
- Find an interest outside oneself.
- Relieve conscious problems in a controlled manner.
- Use opportunities to practice identification, comprehension, and empathy.
- Illuminate difficulties and gain insight into his or her own behavior.

Techniques for Story Time

If possible, apply these ideas when sharing bibliotherapy books with children:

1. **Listen to the children with whom you are sharing the book.**
    - Pay attention.
    - Use eye contact.
    - Observe body clues.
    - Discuss what you think you hear the child saying.
    - Be nonjudgmental.
    - Thank the children for sharing their ideas and feelings.

WHAT IS BIBLIOTHERAPY?

2. **Encourage children to share their feelings with words; support the acceptability of those feelings.**

   - Pay attention.

   - Tell children what you hear them saying: "Right now you hate your best friend."

   - Rephrase children's thoughts in the form of a question: "Are you angry with him?"

   - Help children explore their feelings: "Are you feeling hurt about . . .?"

   - Avoid belittling a child by saying "It's silly to be upset," by telling children how they should be feeling, or by shutting down the conversation, taking over, or saying "Forget it!"

3. **Prepare children for a change or the arrival of a special needs child.**
   Changes are scary when the child or the class does not know what to expect. Prepare for these events with an appropriate book.

   - Begin with a statement that says you are going to be talking and reading about a particular change or situation.

   - Read the book and talk about whatever focus the children wish to pursue.

   - Ask students what they think will happen next.

   - Tell the group what you think might happen and compare how the children's ideas may be similar to or different from yours.

   - Help the children figure out how to adjust to the new situation and plan what they might say or do.

   - If appropriate, practice a hypothetical situation with the group by role playing. Try out several versions with different solutions.

   - Send out an informational letter to parents giving suggestions for things to try at home.

Reference

- *Once Upon a Mind: Using Children's Books to Nurture Self-Discovery*, by Charles A. Smith and Carolyn Lepper Foat. Request single copies from NCR Educational Materials Project, 111N Curtis Hall, Iowa State University, Ames, Iowa 50011.

GENERAL NOTES ON BIBLIOTHERAPY LISTINGS

This list focuses on books for younger children because very few resource lists exist for that age level.

Who publishes reference books on disabilities and impairments?
Several resources are published by R. R. Bowker, 121 Chanlon Road, New Providence, NJ 07974.
- *Accept Me As I Am: Best Book of Juvenile Nonfiction on Impairments and Disabilities.* (1985).
- *Notes from a Different Drummer* (1977) and *More Notes from a Different Drummer: A Guide to Juvenile Fiction Portraying the Handicapped,* by Barbara Baskin and Karen Harris.
- *Portraying Persons with Disabilities: An Annotated Bibliography of Fiction for Children and Teenagers,* by Debra Robertson (1992).

Why are some books annotated while others are not?
Books with older copyright dates are usually not annotated. Newer books are more accessible and are described in current reference literature. An attempt was made to annotate as many books as possible.

Where can teachers and parents find other book lists?
Check with the reference librarian at the public library nearest you. New books that you will want to add to this list come out yearly from publishing companies. A current list is available through the Special Needs Project. (See Chapter 8: Resources and Organizations of Interest.)

What terminology is used in these books?
Terminology varies. Older books may have outdated terms, but the adult reader can change them as he or she reads the book to young children. The illustrations and the way the person with a disability is portrayed are key factors in the decision to read any book. Books with more recent copyright dates tend to use more current terminology.

Are all these books in print?
No, but public libraries will have some of the older titles in their collections because there are so few books for children about disabilities. These books may be located on a parenting shelf or shelved with the subject category. Check the computer or card catalog, or ask the librarian for assistance. If you wish to purchase a book for your own use, check the reference entitled *Books in Print.* Bookstore owners generally can check the availability of a book for you.

Is there a specialty store for this type of book?
Check the resource and organization list for information on the **Special Needs Project,** a mail-order bookstore (phone 800-333-6867, fax 805-683-2341). Also, local resource centers that provide educational services to the disabled may have lending libraries.

GENERAL INTEREST BOOKS ABOUT DISABILITIES

The Discovery Book: A Helpful Guide for the World, Written by Children with Disabilities, by Sky Chaney and Pam Fisher. 1989.

An exploration of the psychosocial aspects of physical disability in youth as expressed by 10- to 15-year-olds with disabilities. This book includes artwork, guided activity sections, and a glossary of terms. Topics include friendship, doctors and hospitals, problems and challenges, goals, wishes and dreams, and coping strategies.

Free to Be . . . You and Me: A Different Kind of Book for Children and Adults to Enjoy Together, by Marlo Thomas and others. McGraw Hill, 1989.

Many articles and stories, each celebrating individual differences with tolerance and good humor.

How It Feels to Fight for Your Life, by Jill Krementz. Little, Brown & Co., 1989.

The introduction makes it clear that this book is not about dying or terminally ill children, but about kids who have faced serious illnesses and disabilities. The author's informants range from 7 to 16 years old, and their statements about life at home and in the hospital with heart disease, spina bifida, severe asthma, and other conditions are straightforward. The excellent photographs are unobtrusive.

How It Feels to Live with a Physical Disability, by Jill Krementz. Simon & Schuster, 1992.

Keith Edward's Different Day, by Karin Melberg Schwier. 1988.

Keith Edward wakes up one morning with the excited anticipation that today will be different, and indeed it is! He meets a man with Down syndrome, a woman using a wheelchair, and a girl who wears a helmet because of seizures. Each person gives Keith a friendly wink. The book is divided into the illustrated story and a parent/teacher discussion guide. The adults with disabilities are portrayed in active, ordinary roles such as shopping and going to work.

Living with a Brother or Sister with Special Needs, by Donald J. Meyer, Patricia F. Vadasy, and Rebecca R. Fewell. University of Washington Press, 1985.

This book gives clear explanations of disabilities as well as tips on how to deal with questions from friends and strangers. In vignettes about typical sibling situations, the authors explore problems in constructive and reassuring ways. Resource listings are included.

GENERAL INTEREST BOOKS ABOUT DISABILITIES

The Survival Guide for Kids with LD, by Gary L. Fisher and Roda E. Cummings. Free Spirit Publications, 1990.

This book describes the experience of growing up with a learning disability from a young person's perspective. Information is based on current research and combined with helpful suggestions to deal with the feelings of being alone. A section is included for parents and teachers.

Understanding the ADA: The Americans with Disabilities Act. 1993.

A pamphlet published by NAEYC, 1509 16th Street NW, Washington, DC 20036-1426

OTHER RESOURCES

Fabric Transfer Patterns and Designs

Kids at Heart (iron-on transfers): Teresa Walsh's drawings reflect cultural and ethnic diversity with characters drawn from people she meets in all walks of life.

I Am Wonderfully Made! (transfer TW30111): Shows an array of disabled children.

Source: SG SO Graphics, Inc.

Video

Let's Be Friends, from Tickle Tune Typhoon, Seattle, Washington, 1989.

Themes of friendship, racial equality, self-health and care, appreciation for different abilities, and environmental awareness form the premise of this video.

AIDS

AIDS: Answers to Questions Kids Ask, by Barbara Christie-Dever. The Learning Works, Inc. 1996.

AIDS: What Teens Need to Know, by Barbara Christie-Dever. The Learning Works, Inc. 1996.
These two activity books teach kids what AIDS is, what causes it, how it's spread, how it can be detected, and more. An easy-to-follow format with extended activities.

Alex, the Kid with AIDS, by Linda Girard. Whitman, 1991.
Michael is in Mrs. Timmer's fourth grade class. Michael and his classmates are informed that a new student, Alex, has AIDS. This book portrays learning experiences for Michael, Alex, Mrs. Timmer, and the class.

Friends for Life, by B. Aisello and J. Shulman. Twenty-First Century, 1988.
This compelling story for young readers examines the strong emotions and feelings of love, loss, anger, and hope that surround the important issues of AIDS. It presents the facts about AIDS in contexts children are familiar with.

Losing Uncle Tim, by Mary Kate Jordan. Whitman, 1989.
Daniel struggles to find reassurance and understanding with his favorite grown-up, Uncle Tim. Uncle Tim, who runs an antique store, is dying of AIDS. Daniel finds that his uncle has left him a legacy of joy and courage plus three special items from the antique store.

ALLERGIES/ASTHMA

Harry's Dog, by Barbara Porte. Greenwillow, 1983.

Harry longs for a pet, but his father is allergic to fur. Harry has a hard time explaining when a dog named Girl is found in his room. The problem of who will keep and care for the dog is solved when Harry's Aunt Rose comes to visit.

Hometown Hero, by B. Aisello and J. Shulman. Twenty-First Century, 1989.

Scott is an active youngster enjoying karate and bike riding. He also is learning to cope with asthma. Bill Waters, a homeless friend of Scott's, plays a part in this story. This book also includes questions and answers about asthma.

I'll Never Love Anything Ever Again, by Judy Delton. Whitman, 1985.

A young boy is faced with giving away his pet, Tinsel, because of allergic reactions.

I'm a Meter Reader, by N. Sander. Allen & Hanburys, 1991.

Itch, Sniffle and Sneeze: All about Asthma, Hay Fever and Other Allergies, by A. Silverstein. Four Winds, New York, 1978.

The Lion Who Had Asthma, by J. London. Whitman, 1992.

Luke Has Asthma, Too, by Alison Rogers, illus. by Michael Middleton. Waterfront, 1987.

This story of Luke gives the message to the reader that asthma can be managed in a calm fashion. A list of resources is included.

So You Have Asthma, Too, by N. Sander. Allen & Hanburys, 1991.

Wheezy, by Michael Charlton. Bodley Head, 1988.

William has asthma that causes physical problems and makes him feel left out of the fun other children have: no pets, no sports, and no friends. William's teacher suggests he start a scrapbook, and the book shows what William drew in his scrapbook.

Winning Over Asthma, by Eileen Dolan Savage. Dolan Press, 1989.

This easy-to-read book for young children tells the story of five-year-old Graham. It describes asthma reactions, triggers, and medicines and shows how parents and doctors can work together.

ALZHEIMER'S/MEMORY LOSS

Always Gramma, by Vaunda Micheaux Nelson. Putnam, 1988.

A little girl is distressed by the changes she sees in her grandmother. She recalls the wonderful times they spent together. Locks are now put on the door so Gramma cannot wander away from home alone. Gramma does not get well, and she is placed in a nursing home. The child is never told the name of the illness, but all of the stages of Alzheimer's disease are in this book.

Georgia Music, by Helen Griffith. Greenwillow, 1986.

A young girl visits her grandfather during the summer months. The first summer is filled with daily routines such as keeping the garden tidy, taking afternoon naps, and playing mouth organ music in the evening. The next summer, the situation changes drastically, and the grandfather is "mighty tired." This book encourages children to interact with others about changes they observe. The ending is left open.

Grandma's Soup, by Nancy Karkowsky. Kar Ben, 1989.

Grampa Doesn't Know It's Me, by Donna Guthrie. Human Sciences, 1986.

Elizabeth's grandfather comes to live with her family when his condition worsens. The book is useful in explaining to very young children the changes Alzheimer's disease causes in adults.

Sachiko Means Happiness, by Kimiko Sakai. Children's Book Press, 1990.

This book shares the experience of a 10-year-old girl caring for her grandmother, who has Alzheimer's. Young Sachiko develops empathy for her grandmother's disorientation and the grandmother's resulting fear of being surrounded by strangers.

Wilfrid Gordon McDonald Partridge, by Mem Fox, illus. by J. Vivas. Kane-Miller, 1985.

Wilfrid Gordon McDonald Partridge lives next door to a nursing home and makes many intergenerational friendships. He especially likes 96-year-old Miss Nancy Alison Delacourt Cooper because she has four names just as he does. He shares secrets with Miss Nancy, and when his parents call her a "poor old thing" who has "lost her memory," Wilfrid sets out to find some memories for her.

APPEARANCE AND SIZE

All Together, One at a Time, by E. Konegsburg. Atheneum, 1971.

Blubber, by J. Blume. Bradbury Press, 1974.

The Ears of Louis, by C. Greene. Viking Press, 1974.

Freckle Juice, by J. Blume. Four Winds Press, 1971.

Hannah the Hippo, by Linda Schwartz. The Learning Works, 1991.
    Hannah is a veterinarian who doesn't like her appearance. As she makes her patients aware of their own good qualities, she realizes that it's what's inside a person that counts.

Much Bigger Than Martin, by S. Kellogg. Dial Press, New York, 1976.

Rosey, The Imperfect Angel, by Sandra Lee Peckinpah. Dosan Productions, 1991.
    This imaginative tale for young children emphasizes the beauty that is hidden beneath physical imperfections. Little Rosey is different from other angels waiting to come to earth, but her difficulties are overcome with the kindly Boss Angel's assistance.

The Shy Little Girl, by P. Kroselovsky. Houghton Mifflin, 1970.

Thinking Big: The Story of a Young Dwarf, by Susan Kuklin. Lothrop, Lee & Shepard, 1986.
    The book, featuring black-and-white photographs by the author, highlights eight-year-old Jaime Osborn, who is an achondroplastic dwarf, which means she has short arms and legs on a normal-size body. This sensitive presentation reveals what Jaime can and cannot do.

The Ugliest Boy, by Robbie Branscum. Lothrop, Lee & Shepard, 1978.

You Look Ridiculous, Said the Rhinoceros to the Hippopotamus, by B. Waber. Houghton Mifflin, 1966.

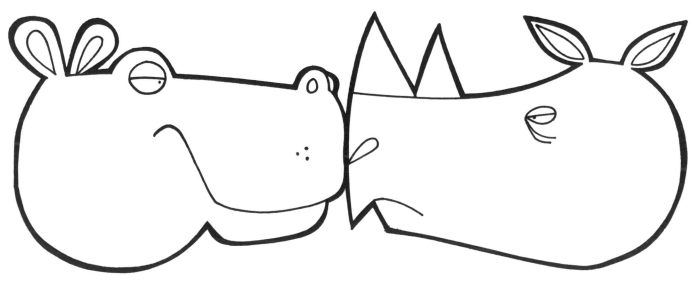

CANCER

Afraid to Ask: A Book about Cancer, by Judylaine Fine. Lothrop, Lee & Shepard, 1986.

Cancer, by Alvin and Virginia Silverstein. Harper and Row, 1977.

Cancer in the Young: A Sense of Hope, by Margaret Hyde and Lawrence Hyde. Westminster, Philadelphia, 1985.

Cancer: The Whispered Word, by Judy Swenson and Roxanne Kunz. Dillon, 1985.

Hang Tough, by Matthew Lancaster. Paulist Press, 1983.

The Hospital Book, by James Howe. Crown, 1981.

I'll Never Walk Alone, by Carol Simonides. Continuum, 1983.

My Book for Kids with Cansur: A Child's Autobiography of Hope, by Jason Gaes. 1987.
   Jason was diagnosed with cancer at the age of six and given a life expectancy of four months. Jason describes the surgery, chemotherapy, and bone marrow tests he endured until remission. This true story, using Jason's own printing and spelling, is an inspirational message to children everywhere on conquering fear, pain, and death. The colorful illustrations are by Jason's brothers.

There's a Little Bit of Me in Jamey, by Diane Amadeo, illus. by J. Friedman. Whitman, 1989.
   Brian, the main character, wakes up one morning to find that his brother has been rushed to the hospital with leukemia. Brian makes his first visit to the hospital, where he has to wear a mask and gown. He observes the intravenous feeding tubes and blood test procedures for Jamey. The story continues with a bone marrow transplant procedure, and Brian is able to help his brother.

CEREBRAL PALSY

Don't Stop the Music, by Robert Perske. Abingdon Press, 1986.
In this novel for young adults, two teen sleuths with cerebral palsy use their critical thinking skills and keen wits to crack an auto theft ring.

Howie Helps Himself, by Jan Fassler. Whitman, 1975.
Expressive drawings show Howie, a school-age child with cerebral palsy, enjoying playing and learning on some days and feeling tired, angry, and clumsy on others. Howie's biggest wish is to be able to move his wheelchair all by himself. Will he be successful?

Joy and the Marigold, by Harriette Gillem Robinet. Children's Press, 1976.
A youngster with cerebral palsy is fascinated by a flower growing in spite of its handicap.

I'm Joshua and "Yes, I Can!" by Joan Lenett. Vantage, 1989.
Joshua is facing the first day of first grade, the "scariest day of his life." His family and teachers help him realize that there are many things he can do and some that he can't do. Joshua has cerebral palsy. The author of the book is Joshua's mother.

I'm the Big Sister Now, by Michelle Emmert, illus. by Gail Owens. Whitman, 1989.
Nine-year-old Michelle writes about family life with her older sister Amy, who was born severely disabled with cerebral palsy. Michelle shows the ways, large and small, that she has become the "big sister."

It's Your Turn at Bat, by B. Aiello and J. Shulman, illus. by Loel Barr. Twenty-First Century, 1988.
The youngster featured in this book, Mark Riley, has cerebral palsy. This engrossing story provides insight into the challenges faced by a person with cerebral palsy. Includes a question and answer section about what it's like to have cerebral palsy.

CYSTIC FIBROSIS

Anna Joins In, by Katrin Arnold, illus. by Renate Seelig. Abingdon, 1983.

Anna has cystic fibrosis, and sometimes her friends make her feel bad because she cannot do everything they can. She wishes she did not have this health problem, especially when her mother has to strike her back to loosen the congestion in her lungs.

Robyn's Book: Growing up with Cystic Fibrosis, by Robyn Miller. Scholastic, 1986.

Through the use of stories, poems, and essays, Robyn Miller shares her thoughts and feelings about growing up with cystic fibrosis.

DEATH AND DYING

Children Are Not Paper Dolls: A Visit with Bereaved Siblings, by Erin Linn Levy (on cancer). Counseling Consultants, Greeley, CO, 1982.

A Gift for Tia Rosa, by Karen Taha. Gemstone, 1986.

Tia Rosa and Tio Juan live next door to eight-year-old Carmelita. Tia Rosa has just come home from the hospital and eventually dies. Carmelita works out her grief by finishing a project that her friend Tia Rosa had begun for a new grandchild.

Gran-Gran's Best Trick: A Story for Children Who Have Lost Someone They Love, by Matthew Galvin. Magination, 1989.

A young girl recalls all the activities she and her grandfather used to do before he became ill with cancer. The book shares insights and information from the girl's parents and her own observations about her grandfather's failing health.

Last Week My Brother Anthony Died, by Martha Hickman. Abingdon, 1984.

Julie is delighted with her new baby brother, but because of his weak heart she is very careful around him once he comes home from the hospital. Julie is able to discuss her feelings of grief and adjustment after Anthony dies.

The Saddest Time, by Norma Simon. Whitman, 1986.

This book contains three different short stories about terminal illnesses. It is intended to help young children who may be confused by television and movie scenes in which an actor dies and then seemingly comes to life again on another program.

A Time for Remembering, by Chuck Thurman. Simon & Schuster, 1989.

A young boy visits his grandfather in the hospital. After the grandfather's death, the boy honors his grandfather's last request. This book portrays the honoring of that wish in a sensitive way, along with showing the hospitalized person as approachable instead of in quarantine.

DIABETES

A Portrait of Me, by B. Aiello and J. Shulman. Twenty-First Century, 1989.
  This young adult fiction book is about Ellis Island, a girl named Christine, and her love of modern dance and Greek food. Her challenge is living with diabetes.

Touch Beans, by Betty Bates, illus. by Leslie Morrill. Holiday, 1988.
  Nat collapses playing baseball and finds out that he has diabetes. His fourth-grade year is filled with complications. Nat learns to cope with Jasper, the class bully, and with diet restrictions and medication, plus the move of his best friend, Cassie.

DOWN SYNDROME/MENTAL DISABILITIES

Be Good to Eddie Lee, by V. Fleming, illus. by F. Cooper. Putnam & Grosset, 1993.
  A summer day's outing to search for frog eggs is the setting for the special story of Eddie Lee, a child with Down syndrome. He forms a friendship with two other youngsters, Christy and Jim Bud.

Making Room for Uncle Joe, by Ada Litchfield, illus. by G. Owens. Whitman, 1984.
  Uncle Joe comes to live with his sister's family and his nephew, Dan. This book describes the family's concerns, apprehensions, and adjustments. Joe, an adult with Down syndrome, becomes part of the family and is asked to stay. This book addresses in a positive way some stereotypes about adults with mental disabilities.

My Brother Steven Is Retarded, by Harriet Sobol. Includes photographs. Macmillan, 1977.
  The illustrations and straightforward text describe eleven-year-old Beth's often conflicting feelings toward her older brother. Youngsters with brothers or sisters will recognize these feelings.

My Friend Jacob, by Lucille Clifton. Dutton, 1980.

My Sister, by Karen Hirsch. Carolrhoda Books, 1977.

My Sister Is Different, by Betty Ren Wright. Raintree, 1981.
  Carlo has a lot of resentment about being in charge of his older sister, Terry. She acts younger than Carlo because of her mental impairment. Other children make fun of Terry, and Carlo sometimes finds it hard to follow his grandmother's advice to love his sister.

Our Brother Has Down Syndrome: An Introduction for Children, by Shelley Cairo. Photographs by Irene McNeil. Annick Press, Toronto, Canada, 1985.
  Large color photographs and a sensitive text describe two sisters' lives with their younger brother, who has Down syndrome. Presents clear, concise information about Down syndrome.

A Special Kind of Sister, by Lucia Smith. Henry Holt, 1979.
  At seven, Sarah is coping with feelings about her younger brother, who is mentally impaired. He gets attention, he embarrasses her in public, and most of all, Sarah is afraid she will lose her friends. Mom tries to help Sarah focus on the ways she is special.

DOWN SYNDROME/MENTAL DISABILITIES

Stay Away from Simon! by Carol Carrick. Clarion, 1985.
A mentally disabled boy assists two children, Lucy and Josiah, when they become lost in a snowstorm while walking home from school. The setting is in Martha's Vineyard in the 1830s. An excellent book for helping children understand their fears concerning others who seem "different."

Where's Chimpy? by Bernice Rabe. Whitman, 1988.
Chimpy, a favorite bedtime cuddle toy, can't be found one night, and even Dad helps look. Chimpy's owner has Down syndrome, and the reader will delight in the ending.

EPILEPSY

Edith Herself, by Ellen Howard. Atheneum, 1987.
Edith goes to live with her oldest sister, Alena, and brother-in-law, John. There, she will be raised with her cousin, Vernon. The story is set in the late 1800s when epilepsy is looked on with shame and ignorance. Edith helps her peers develop tolerance, just as she herself learns tolerance toward an older female relative.

Halsey's Pride, by Lynn Hall. Scribner, 1990.

A Handful of Stars, by Barbara Girion. Scribner, 1981.

Lee, The Rabbit with Epilepsy, by Deborah M. Moss. Woodbine House, 1989.
Lee, a small bunny, is diagnosed with epilepsy. Lee is scared, but the doctor and Lee's family are supportive as they explain what it means and how the little bunny will continue to do her favorite activities, even though she has a medical disability.

Madeline and the Great (Old) Escape Artist, by Rebecca Jones. Dutton, 1983.
Madeline meets Mary Gibson during a hospital stay. The two make plans to live together in the city. When the plans fall apart, both make new decisions with courage.

Run, Patty, Run, by Sheila Cragg. Harper & Row, 1980.

A Season of Secrets, by Allison Cragen Herzip. Little, Brown & Co., 1982.

Trick or Treat or Trouble, by B. Aiello and J. Shulman. Twenty-First Century, 1989.
This story depicts a Halloween event that features Brian, a youngster with epilepsy. An informative question-and-answer section on epilepsy is included in this book.

What Difference Does It Make, Danny? by Helen Young. Andre Deutsch, 1981.

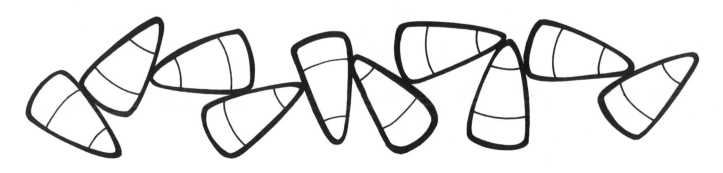

HEARING AND SIGNING

A Button in Her Ear, by Ada Litchfield. Whitman, 1976.

Angela is a school-age child who keeps misinterpreting what people say to her. Expressive drawings convey Angela's confusion and frustration prior to the diagnosis of her hearing impairment and show her adjustment as she gains a sense of control by caring for her own hearing aid.

Amy, The Story of a Deaf Child, by Lou Ann Walker. Photographs by Michael Abramson. 1990.

Amy is a fifth-grade girl who is deaf. She communicates in sign and spoken language and uses hearing aids, lip reading, and interpreters to understand what people are saying. A list of resources for the deaf follows the story.

Chris Gets Ear Tubes, by Elizabeth Pace. Gallaudet University Press, 1987.

Chris cannot hear well because of fluid in his ears. He goes to the hospital to have ear tubes inserted. Chris is taken on a hospital tour and rides on a gurney and in a wheelchair. His family is there to encourage him, and the operation is a success.

Discovering Sign Language, by Laura Greene and Eva Barash Dicker. Gallaudet University Press, 1988.

Children learn about the use of sign language to communicate and about various devices for the hearing impaired. Games and activities are highlighted.

Handtalk, An ABC of Finger Spelling and Sign Language, by Remy Charlip and Mary Miller. Four Winds, Macmillan, 1984.

Actress-teacher Mary Beth and other members of the National Theater of the Deaf scamper through the alphabet in George Ancona's full-page color photographs.

Handtalk Birthday, A Number and Story Book in Sign Language, by Remy Charlip, Mary Miller, and George Ancona. Macmillan, 1991.

The setting of this book is Mary Beth's surprise birthday party, and the book depicts the spontaneous fun of such an event.

Handtalk Zoo, by Mary Beth and George Ancona. Macmillan, 1989.

Five energetic young guides take you on a colorful trip to the zoo, all in sign language.

I Can Sign my ABC's, by Susan Gibbons Chaplin. Gallaudet University Press, 1986.

I Can't Always Hear You, by Joy Zelonky. Raintree, 1980.

Kim, a 10-year-old with a hearing aid, tells of her adjustments to a mainstreamed classroom and her struggles with the way other classmates treat her. This story encourages readers to consider the special qualities of all people.

I Have a Sister, My Sister is Deaf, by J. Peterson. Harper & Row, 1984.

The narrator, a young girl, describes the positive and negative aspects of her deaf sister's life at home. The book emphasizes to the reader that although being deaf doesn't hurt, her sister's feelings are hurt when people don't understand her problem. The text and illustrations provide a warm, tender portrayal of sibling love.

HEARING AND SIGNING

I Hear, by R. Isadora. Greenwillow, 1985.

I Hear, by Helen Oxenbury. Random House, 1986.

I'm Deaf and It's Okay, by Lorraine Aseltine and Evelyn Mueller. Whitman, 1986.
   When a young boy realizes that he will always have to wear hearing aids, he rebels. A teenager who is deaf helps the boy understand that he will be able to have an active adult life. The plot is simple but provides a good description of the fears, frustrations, and satisfactions of the hearing impaired.

Lisa and Her Soundless World, by Enda S. Levine. Human Sciences, 1984.
   This story focuses on Lisa, an eight-year-old girl who was born deaf, and on the difficulties she experiences in a hearing world. New vistas open for her as her parents recognize that she is deaf. New adaptive communication tools are made available to her. The text includes descriptions for hearing children to help them understand what it is like to be deaf.

Mandy, by Barbara D. Booth, illus. by Jim Lamarche. Lothrop, Lee & Shepard, 1991.
   This book provides a rare insight into the world of a deaf child and her special relationship with her grandmother. A missing silver pin challenges Mandy to conquer her fear of the dark.

My First Book of Sign, by Pamela Baker. Gallaudet University Press, 1986.
   This book for hearing children about deaf people's language will open the door to new forms of communication.

My Sister's Silent World, by Catherine Arthur. Children's Press, 1979.
   A young girl describes the world of her eight-year-old deaf sister. Lively photographs of the sisters add to the appeal. This tale can be read aloud to a class as an introduction to deafness.

Nursery Rhymes from Mother Goose Told in Signed English, by Harry Bornstein and Karen Saulnier. Gallaudet University Press, 1992.
   Twelve popular nursery rhymes are illustrated with delightful pictures and clear sign language directions.

Sesame Street Sign Language ABC, by Linda Bove. Random House, 1986.

Sesame Street Sign Language Fun, by Linda Bove. Random House, 1980.

Silent Lotus, by Jeanne Lee. Farrar, Straus, & Giroux, 1991.

Words in Our Hands, by Ada Litchfield. Whitman, 1980.
   A young boy shares his experiences growing up with deaf parents. The book presents in a sensitive way the family dynamics as well as some of the frustrations the boy feels. It gives excellent explanations of why some people are difficult to understand and how some forms of hearing impairment occur.

LEARNING DISABILITIES

The Beast in Ms. Rooney's Room, by Patricia Reilly Giff. Dell, 1984.

A young boy named Richard Best, who calls himself "Beast," is repeating the second grade. He makes friends with the best speller in the class, and a breakthrough occurs in his behavior and in his learning ability. This is part of a series of books suitable for the early grades.

Different, Not Dumb, by Margot Marek. Franklin Watts, 1985.

Mike is in the second grade. Math is not a problem, but reading is quite difficult. His learning disability is addressed once he begins a special class for remedial reading exercises. Mike becomes a hero just by reading an important word.

The Flunking of Joshua T. Bates, by Susan Shreve. Knopf, 1984.

The day before school starts, Joshua gets the bad news that he will have to repeat third grade. His behavior turns disruptive. His situation improves through the use of support services. The text uses the terminology of learning differences. The story is humorous, but children who have learning disabilities that cannot be dispelled so readily as Joshua's may be disappointed.

Herbie Jones, by Suzy Kline. Putnam, 1985.

This book addresses the dilemma of names for reading groups. Herbie is in the third grade with the typical peer situations. The story is funny and just right for eager new readers looking for a series.

Josh, by Caroline Janover, illus. by Edward Epstein. 1988.

This story, written by an educator, shares personal experiences about dyslexia. It is the story of Josh, a fifth grader who meets the challenges of classroom life.

The Misunderstood Child: A Guide for Parents of Children with Learning Disabilities, second edition, by L. Silver. McGraw Hill, 1991.

Someone Special, Just Like You, by T. Brown. Holt Rhinehart & Winston, 1984.

Through the use of photographs and text, children are shown doing all the favorite things that children like to do: playing on playgrounds, eating ice cream, giving hugs, etc. It is incidental that all the children shown have a special need.

Secrets Aren't (Always) for Keeps, by B. Aiello and J. Shulman. Twenty-First Century, 1988.

Jennifer finds it difficult to keep her learning disability a secret from her classmates. This delightful story is about believing in oneself and knowing that secrets aren't always for keeps. A question-and-answer section follows the story.

LEUKEMIA, SEE CANCER

MISCELLANEOUS

EMOTIONAL DISTRESS

Mama One, Mama Two, by Patricia MacLachlan. Harper & Row, 1982.
A foster parent helps a youngster understand that a child can have two caregivers and loving relationships with both mamas.

Miss Nelson Has a Field Day, by Harry Allard. Houghton Mifflin, 1985.
Everyone at Horace B. Smedley School has been down in the dumps because the football team is really bad. The children are subdued, and the principal is "so depressed he hid under his desk." The Miss Nelson series of books provides humorous plots and a hint of mystery. This book acknowledges that stress can affect the entire population of a school in different ways.

LEFT-HANDEDNESS

Lefty, by Marguerite Rush Lerner. Lerner Publications, 1960.

MULTIPLE DISABILITIES

Don't Feel Sorry for Paul, by Bernard Wolf. Lippincott, 1974.
Though born without complete arms and legs, Paul is becoming a self-sufficient person. The book illustrates his everyday tasks such as getting dressed, taking a horseback-riding lesson, and coping with a typical day at elementary school.

My Friend Leslie: A Story of a Handicapped Child, by Maxine B. Rosenberg. Photographs by George Ancona. Lothrop, Lee & Shepard, 1983.
A kindergarten girl narrates this story about her special friendship with Leslie, a classmate with multiple physical disabilities. Her description of their friendship and of their first school year addresses many of the questions and feelings that are likely to arise when children or adults meet someone with multiple disabilities for the first time.

MISCELLANEOUS

MULTIPLE SCLEROSIS

My Mommy's Special, by Jennifer English. Children's Press, 1985.
Sometimes it's parents who have the disability and the children who need to adjust to the life situation. This photo picture book shows Jennifer's mom with multiple sclerosis and in a wheelchair. The text is in primary print and suitable as a beginner's reading book.

The Snailman, by Brenda Silvers. Little, Brown & Co., 1978.

PHYSICAL/ORTHOPEDIC IMPAIRMENTS

Button Eye's Orange, by Jan Wahl. Warner, 1980.
A special bond forms between Bonzer, a boy with braces, and a stuffed animal named Button Eye, which has a leg sewn on backward. Going to the market for an orange sets the scene for an adventure. This story also shows a single parent family.

DinnieAbbieSister-r-r! by Riki Levinson. Four Winds, 1987.
Two brothers and their preschool sister have a great relationship in a lively Jewish family living in Bensonhurst, Brooklyn. When the mother wants one of them to come home, she always calls out "DinnieAbbieSister-r-r!" When Abbie becomes too ill to go to school, the two siblings adjust to changes that the unnamed illness brings, including therapy sessions.

Grandma Drives a Motor Bed, by Diane Hamm Johnson. Whitman, 1987.
Grandma is an invalid being cared for by Grandpa. Joel is aware of the frustrations and limitations in his grandparents' lives, but he enjoys his interaction with them and takes special pleasure in being allowed to use the controls of the motor bed.

Harry and Willy and Carrothead, by Judith Caseley. Greenwillow, 1991.
Born without a hand, Harry's parents accept him with delight. At four, Harry is fitted for a prosthesis, and at five, he handles new classmates' curiosity in a friendly way. Harry's parents set the tone of an accepting attitude that readers will absorb. Harry's baseball skills are an inspiration.

A Honey of a Chimp, by Norma Klein. Pantheon, 1980.

The Little Lame Prince, by Rosemary Wells. Dial Books, 1990.

My Great Grandpa, by Martin Waddell. Putnam, 1990.

Now One Foot, Now the Other, by Tomie de Paola. Putnam, 1981.

Patrick and Emma Lou, by Nan Holcomb. Jason & Nordic Publications, 1989.

MISCELLANEOUS

PHYSICAL/ORTHOPEDIC IMPAIRMENTS

Ride the Red Cycle, by Harriette Gilliam Robinet. Houghton Mifflin, 1980.
At two, Jerome developed meningitis, which left him with long-term physical disabilities. Now eleven, he wants to ride a bicycle. Does Jerome's dream come true? The book gives a sensitive presentation of the feelings of a youngster with disabilities who wants a chance to succeed and of a sibling's feelings of anger, sympathy, and love.

Ty's One-Man Band, by Mildred Pitts Walter. Four Winds, 1980.

The Wall, by Eve Bunting. Houghton Mifflin, 1990.
Simple text conveys impressions and information related to the Vietnam Memorial. A disabled veteran without legs is one of the visitors to the memorial, along with a teacher and her class.

VISION

Apartment 3, by Ezra Jack Keats. Macmillan, 1971.

Business Is Looking Up, by B. Aiello and J. Shulman. Twenty-First Century Books, 1989.
Renaldo Rodriquex is a lively 11-year-old who has been visually impaired since birth. Renaldo learns that there is more to running a business than just making money.

Cakes and Miracles, by Barbara Goldin. Viking, 1990.
Hershel is blind and prays for a way to be of more help (a Purim tale).

A Cane in Her Hand, by Ada B. Litchfield, illus. by Eleanor Mill. Whitman, 1977.
This moving story describes the reactions of peers and strangers as well as Valerie's own feelings of fear, anger, and pride as she learns to walk with a cane and cope with her disability.

Catching, by Virginia Allen Jensen. Philomel Books, 1983.
This books tells a story of Little Rough, who plays tag and many other fun games. The text is printed, but the pictures and page numbers are raised to be felt or seen. This book is great for blind or sighted youngsters.

A Guide Dog Puppy Grows Up, by Caroline Arnold. Harcourt Brace, 1991.
This delightful photo book follows Honey, a young golden retriever, as she becomes a student at Guide Dogs for the Blind in San Rafael, California. It answers all the questions that children have about how the dogs learn to stop at stop lights, navigate crowded streets, and do all the other helpful acts for their blind partners.

Happy Birthday, Grampie, by Susan Pearson. Dial, 1987.
Grampie, Martha's blind Swedish grandfather, is living in a nursing home. Martha has prepared a special card made from textured paper to spell out the birthday message. Grampie puzzles over the card, then smiles and responds in English that he loves Martha.

VISION

I See, by R. Isadora. Greenwillow, 1985.

I See, by Helen Oxenbury. Random House, 1986.

Knots on a Counting Rope, by Bill Martin and John Archambault, illus. by Ted Rand. Henry Holt and Company, 1987.
    Boy, a Native American, sits near the campfire and encourages his Navaho grandfather to tell once again the stories of his birth and early life. This warm story shares culture, love, and support for a child born blind.

My Favorite Place, by Susan Sargent & D. A. Wirt. Abingdon Press, 1983.
    This story shares a family's day at the beach. It is only on the last pages that the reader is told that the girl who has been having so much fun has been blind all her life.

The Potato Man, by Megan McDonald. Orchard, 1991.
    Grandfather tells how, as a child, he and the neighborhood kids were frightened of the vegetable seller, Mr. Angelo, who had lost an eye in the Great War.

See You Tomorrow, Charles, by Miriam Cohen, illus. by Lillian Hoban. Greenwillow, 1983.
    The new student in the first-grade class is blind. The story unfolds from the perspective of Charles' sighted classmates by sharing their feelings and activities. The blind child, Charles, is portrayed as capable but with a quiet personality.

Seven Blind Mice, by Ed Young. Philomel, 1992.
    A Caldecott Award book that illustrates an old folk tale with a moral.

Through Grandpa's Eyes, by Patricia MacLachlan. Harper & Row, 1980.
    This tender story describes a special relationship. John and his grandfather are inseparable. They exercise, play the cello, and go for walks. John has a different view of the world, as seen though the eyes of his blind grandfather.

WHEELCHAIR USE

Apple Pie and Onions, by J. Caseley, Greenwillow, 1987.
Rebecca and her grandmother buy apples for a pie. Later, Rebecca's grandmother stops by a friend's wheelchair and chats; Rebecca is embarrassed and insists that the conversation stop. Grandma tells her a story about the time her father embarrassed her on the subway by wearing dirty work clothes and carrying a sack of smelly onions. Once home, Grandma's father kissed her, and her mother used the onions in a stew. Rebecca resolves her discomfort, and the apple pie is one of the best ever.

Arnie and the New Kid, by Nancy Carlson. Viking Press, 1990.
Everybody at school is a little bit afraid of Philip because he is different from them. Only one person, Arnie, teases Philip. One day Arnie's teasing gets out of hand and leads to an accident that puts Arnie off his feet, just like Philip. Arnie discovers you can be different and still be alike, and he learns what friendship is all about.

The Balancing Girl, by Bernice Rabe, illus. by Lillian Hoban. Dutton, 1981.
Margaret, a first grader, uses leg braces, crutches, or a wheelchair. Her disability is clearly portrayed in color drawings but not singled out in the text. Margaret's disposition is sunny, and she enjoys life in a typical classroom. Margaret comes up with a spectacular idea for a school fair.

Grandma's Wheelchair, by Lorraine Henriod, illus. by Christa Chevalier. Whitman, 1982.
Four-year-old Tomas spends his mornings helping his grandmother, who is in a wheelchair. This story emphasizes the grandmother's matter-of-fact capabilities and independent view of life.

Mama Zooms, by Jane Cowen-Fletcher. Scholastic, 1993.
A young child rides along when Mama uses her wheelchair. Delightful illustrations are accompanied by limited text.

Move Over, Wheelchairs Coming Through, by R. Roy. Clarion, 1985.
Seven young people, ages eight to nineteen, overcome the constraints imposed by the disabled bodies that house their active minds.

My Buddy, by Audrey Osofsky, illus. by Ted Rand. Henry Holt & Company, 1992.
Buddy is a golden retriever that "works" for a boy in a wheelchair. His training as well as his care and the many things he can do for his owner are presented in a very positive way.

Nick Joins In, by Joe Lasker. Whitman, 1980.
Nick, who uses a wheelchair, faces his first day of kindergarten. The story describes Nick's worries about school.

No Trouble for Grandpa, by Carol Marron. Raintree, 1983.
David and his younger sister spend an overnight visit at Grandpa's house. During a shopping trip, an incident occurs that puts the focus on David's ability to provide help for his sister, Amy. David is in a wheelchair.

WHEELCHAIR USE

One Light, One Sun, by Raffi. Crown, 1988.

Raffi's song lyrics are illustrated by an integrated population of families. Skin tones vary, and cross-generational relations are established. One child is dependent on a wheelchair and adult assistance.

Our Teacher's in a Wheelchair, by M. Powers. Whitman, 1986.

Brian Hanson, a young teacher injured in a lacrosse accident, now teaches from a wheelchair. This photo essay book follows him through a typical day, focusing on his interactions with children in the day-care setting where he works. The story takes place in Oakland, California.

Princess Pooh, by Kathleen M. Maldoon. Whitman, 1989.

Patty Jean Piper calls her older sister Penny "Princess Pooh." The name comes from her sister's sitting on her "wheelchair-throne" all day long, telling other people, especially Patty Jean, what to do. One day Patty Jean tries out her sister's wheelchair and has a string of problems. A new relationship results, and Patty gains empathy for her sister's situation.

A Very Special Critter, by Gina and Mercer Mayer. Western, 1993.

This is one of the inexpensive, full-color "critter" series books done by Mercer Mayer. Alex, the new critter kid in class, uses a wheelchair. Other school critters are curious. Alex turns out to be "cool" and just one of the gang.

With the Wind, by Liz Damrell. Orchard Books, 1991.

Through poetry, a boy's ride on horseback is described. It is only at the end that the reader discovers that the unnamed boy also rides in a wheelchair. The book features the Heads Up riding program for disabled children.

CHAPTER 8
RESOURCES AND ORGANIZATIONS OF INTEREST

WHERE TO GET HELP

A good place to begin seeking information is from your local school district's special services department.

For copies of legislation related to special education in your state, write to the State Department of Education in your state's capital. For example, in California write to the State Department of Education, 721 Capital Mall, Sacramento, CA 95814.

Health Resource Directory   800-544-3284
American Council on Education, Health Resource Center
One Dupont Circle, Washington, DC 20036-1193

The Health Resource Center is a clearing house that operates under a Congressional legislative mandate to collect and disseminate information nationally about disability issues in post-secondary education. It publishes a free biannual resource guide organized under the following topics: advocacy, access, and awareness; community integration; disability-specific organizations; funding; legal assistance; and technology. An outstanding resource!

Special Needs Project   805-683-9633
3463 State Street, Suite 282, Santa Barbara, CA 93105

This unique, comprehensive bookstore started by Hod Grey provides a gamut of books that address the needs of young children through the seasoned professional. Books are available by mail, phone, fax, and e-mail. A catalog is in progress and will be available on disk and audio tape as well as on Apple's e/World information service. This bookstore has a complete inventory and a knowledgeable staff.

Advocacy Manual:
A Parent's How-to Guide for Special Education Services
4156 Library Road, Pittsburgh, PA 15243

Write to the above address to order this 1992 manual produced by the LDA Advocacy Committee.

WHERE TO GET HELP

Captioned Films/Videos from Modern Talking Picture Service, Inc.   800-237-6213
5000 Park Street North, St. Petersburg, FL 33709

This company provides free loans of educational and general interest films and videos. The program is made available by the U.S. Department of Education, Office of Special Education. Users of 16-mm films are required to pay return postage. One-half-inch VHS videos with prepaid return postage labels included in the cassette cases are absolutely free to use. An application process must be completed prior to use. Request applications and brochures from the company.

Center on Human Policy/Early Childhood Direction Center   315-443-3851
200 Huntington Hall, Second Floor, Syracuse, NY 13244

Computer Resources for People with Disabilities: A Guide to Exploring Today's Assistive Technology, by Alliance for Technology Access, Hunter House, 1994.

Foundation for Technology Access   415-455-4575
2173 East Francisco Blvd., Suite L, San Rafael, CA 94901
Order by phone, e-mail: ATA FTA@AOL.COM, or fax: 415-455-0654.

Disabilities Statistics Research and Training Center   415-502-5210

Closer Look, Parents' Campaign for Handicapped Children and Youth
Box 1492, Washington, DC 20013

Responds to most inquiries by sending out packets of information tailored to the requester's information needs, such as lists of state agencies, local parent groups, organizations serving specific disabilities, legal rights, and parent advocacy.

ERIC Clearinghouse on Disabilities and Gifted Education   800-328-0272
Council for Exceptional Children 1920 Association Drive, Reston, VA 22091-1589

This clearinghouse gathers and disseminates educational information on all disabilities and on gifted children across all age levels. It provides the following services: acquiring, selecting, abstracting, and indexing professional literature. Referral information is provided to users.

Learning Styles Resource: Academic Therapy Publications   805-654-6400, Ext. 1244
Dr. Jeffrey Barsch, Learning Disabilities Specialist
Ventura Community College, Ventura, CA 93003

WHERE TO GET HELP

National Association for the Education of Young Children   800-424-2460
1509 16th Street NW, Washington, DC 20036
   NAEYC offers resources and services to early childhood professionals, parents, and policymakers about child development and early education. Their bimonthly journal, *Young Children*, offers the latest information in early childhood research, theory, and practice.

News Digest, National Information Center for Children and Youth with Disabilities 800-695-0285
Box 1492, Washington, DC 20013
   NICHCY provides free information in English and Spanish to assist parents, educators, caregivers, advocates, and others to help children and youth with disabilities participate as fully as possible in school, at home, and in the community. NICHCY can also provide personal responses to specific questions. Single copies of NICHCY materials are free. Permission to duplicate NICHCY materials is not required; simply credit NICHCY as the source of the material.

Resource Networks, Inc.   708-864-4522
1618 Orrington Avenue, Evanston, IL 60201
   Dr. Ken Moses, a psychologist, provides informational tapes and presentations on issues and sensitive topics that parents of children with disabilities face, such as death and the grieving process.

NEWSPAPERS AND MAGAZINES

- *Accent on Living,* Box 700, Bloomington, IL 61701, 309-378-2961
- *Closing the Gap,* P.O. Box 68, Henderson, MN 56044, 612-248-3294
- *Child Care Information Exchange,* P.O. Box 2890, Redmond, WA 98073
- *Child Health Alert,* P.O. Box 338, Newton Highlands, MA 02161
- *Disability Rag,* Box 145, Louisville, KY 40201
- *Exceptional Parent,* 605 Commonwealth Avenue, Boston, MA 02215, 617-536-8961
- *Mainstream,* 2973 Beech Street, San Diego, CA 92102, 619-234-3138
- *Parents' Pediatric Report,* Box 155, 77 Ives Street, Providence, RI 02906

BOOKS

Computers and the Americans with Disabilities Act: A Manager's Guide, by John A. McCormick. McGraw-Hill, Inc., 1994.
This comprehensive book covers all aspects of computers and information for people with disabilities.

KITS AND MATERIALS DESIGNED FOR CLASSROOM USE

Friends Who Care: A Teachers' Kit from Easter Seals   800-221-6827
70 East Lake Street, Chicago, IL 60601
The National Easter Seal Society has put out a curriculum that provides information about teaching nondisabled students to accept and include their peers with disabilities in school and everyday activities. Resources galore are available in the catalog.

Heart Treasure Chest and Getting to Know Your Heart   800-AHA-USA1
The American Heart Association has three comprehensive curriculum programs aimed at preschool through the middle grades, designed to develop positive heart health habits related to diet, physical activity, and rest. Contact your local Heart Association for details and cost.

Kid Love Unlimited   714-643-9422
2973 Harbor Blvd., #508, Costa Mesa, CA 92626
Contains a potpourri of materials on awareness and appreciation of learning differences. Kid Love was started by Kathleen Morey, a mother who organizes parent support groups and workshops. A *Kid Love* catalog is a must for anyone working with a child with special needs.

Kids on the Block: A Puppet Presentation   800-368-5437
Kids on the Block groups are organized nationwide by volunteers delivering the message of disability awareness with presentations using lifelike puppets. This organization provides training, puppets, skits, and support materials for volunteer groups. The two-part presentation consists of a puppet presentation the first week, followed by a visit from a guest speaker with a disability who will answer questions during the second week.

Understanding Handicaps, from Newton, Inc.   617-552-7687
This disability-awareness curriculum written for classroom volunteers to use with fourth-grade students includes simulation activities, activity demonstrations, various aids and adaptive equipment, audio-visual materials, printed materials, and bibliographies.

PLAY EQUIPMENT SUPPLIERS

- **Rifton Equipment and Community Playthings,** Route 213, Rifton, NY 12471   800-777-4244
Designs and produces play equipment for children who are disabled.
- **Crestwood Co.,** 6625 North Sydney Place, Milwaukee, WI 53209   414-352-5678
Provides specially adapted toys for children with special needs.
- **The Fibar Group,** 141 Halstead Avenue, Mamaroneck, NY 10543   800-342-2721
Manufactures playground surfaces that make play areas accessible for children using wheelchairs, crutches, or walkers.
- **Jesana Ltd.,** Box 17, Irvington, NY 10533   800-443-4728
Makes adapted toys and equipment for children with disabilities.

800 NUMBERS

ADA Helpline at the Equal Employment Opportunity Commission 800-669-EEOC
Alzheimer's Association 800-272-3900
American Association on Mental Retardation 800-424-3688
American Cancer Society 800-ACS-2345
American Council of the Blind 800-424-8666
American Diabetes Association 800-232-3472
American Foundation for the Blind 800-232-5463
American Heart Association 800-AHA-USA1
American Liver Foundation 800-223-0179
American Printing House for the Blind 800-223-1839
American Speech-Language-Hearing Association 800-638-8255
Amyotrophic Lateral Sclerosis (ALS) Association 800-782-4747
Arthritis Foundation 800-283-7800
Asthma and Allergy Foundation of America 800-727-8462
Autism Society of America 800-3AUTISM
Cancer Information Service 800-4-CANCER
Captioned Films for the Deaf . . . . .800-237-6213, Voice/TDD
Children's Craniofacial Association 800-535-3643
Children's Hospice International 800-242-4453
Cleft Palate Foundation 800-24-CLEFT

800 NUMBERS

Cornelia de Lange Syndrome Foundation 800-223-8355
Council of Citizens with Low Vision 800-733-2258
Crohn's and Colitis Foundation of America 800-343-3637
Cystic Fibrosis Foundation 800-344-4823
Education Resource Project 800-487-6530
Epilepsy Foundation of America 800-332-1000
Family Survival Project 800-445-8106
Federal Student Aid Information Center 800-433-3243
Health Resource Center 800-544-3284
Hearing Helpline 800-327-9355
Hear Now, National Hearing Aid Bank ....800-648-HEAR Voice/TDD
Huntington's Disease Society 800-345-4372
Immune Deficiency Foundation 800-296-4433
Info Tech 800-331-3027
International Hearing Aid Society Helpline 800-521-5247
Job Accommodation Network 800-526-7234
Juvenile Diabetes Association 800-223-1138
Library of Congress Handicapped Hotline 800-424-8567
Lupus Foundation Information Line 800-558-0121
Modern Talking Picture Services, Inc. 800-237-6213
Multiple Sclerosis 24-Hour Information Line 800-344-4867
National Adoption Center for Special Needs and Physically Disabled Children 800-TO-ADOPT
National Center for the Blind 800-638-7518

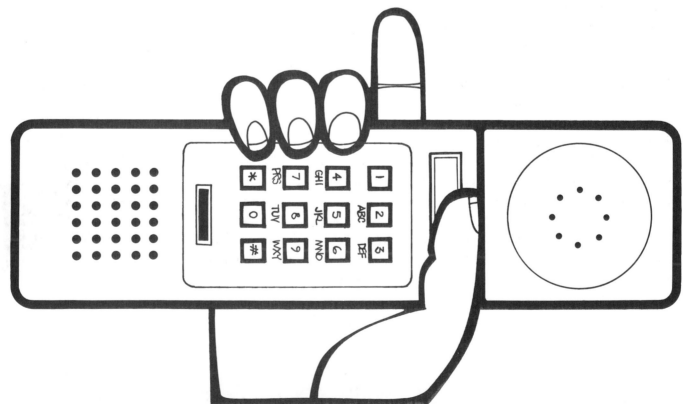

800 NUMBERS

Centers for Disease Control HIV and AIDS Hotline .800-342-2437
National AIDS Hotlines
    Deaf 800-AIDS-TTY
    English 800-342-2437
    Spanish 800-344-SIDA
National Alliance for the Mentally Ill Helpline 800-950-6264
National Alliance of Blind Students 800-424-8666
National Brain Injury Foundation Family Helpline .800-444-6443
National Center for Youth with Disabilities 800-333-6293
National Clearinghouse of Rehabilitation Training Materials 800-223-5219
National Down Syndrome Congress 800-232-NDSC
National Down Syndrome Society 800-221-4602
National Easter Seal Society 800-221-6827
National Health Information Center 800-336-4797
National Hospice Organization Helpline 800-658-8898
National Information System and Clearinghouse for Infants with Disabilities 800-922-9234
National Institute on Deafness and Other Communication Disorders 800-241-1044
National Kidney Foundation Information Center 800-622-9010
National Mental Health Consumer Self-Help Clearinghouse 800-553-4539
National Neurofibromatosis Foundation 800-323-7938
National Organization for Rare Disorders 800-999-6673
National Organization on Disability 202-293-5960
National Rehabilitation Information Center 800-346-2742
National Reyes Syndrome Foundation 800-233-7393
National Spinal Cord Injury Association 800-962-9629
National Spinal Cord Injury Hotline 800-526-3456
Orton Dyslexia Society 800-222-3123
Short Stature Foundation Helpline 800-243-9273
Spina Bifida Association 800-621-3141
Stuttering Foundation of America 800-992-9392
Tourette Syndrome Association 800-237-0717
United Cerebral Palsy 800-872-5827
United Leukodystrophy Foundation 800-728-5483
United Ostomy Association 800-826-0826

Note: Some 800 numbers will not work within an organization's local area. Organizations offer 800 numbers to increase accessibility. Calls are charged to the organization and, thus, are not truly free.

ASSISTIVE COMPUTER TECHNOLOGY RESOURCES

The following general suppliers are listed for your convenience.

AbleNet, Inc., 1081 Tenth Avenue SE, Minneapolis, MN 55414 .612-379-0956

Academic Software, 331 West Second Street, Lexington, KY 40507 606-233-2332

Adap Tech, 2501 North Loop Drive, Ames, IA 50010 515-296-7171

Alliance for Technology Access

   2173 East Francisco Blvd., Suite L, San Rafael, CA 94901 415-455-4575

Berkeley Systems, Inc., 2095 Rose Street, Berkeley, CA 94709 510-540-5535

Deaf and Disabled Telecommunications Program, GTE-Pacific Bell 800-821-2585
   P.O. Box 1013, Norwalk, CA 90651

Don Johnston Developmental Equipment 708-526-2682
   1000 North Rand Road, Building 115
   P.O. Box 639, Wauconda, IL 60084

Edmark Corporation, P.O. Box 3218, Redmond, WA 98073-3218 800-426-0856

Educational Resources, 1550 Executive Drive, Elgin, IL 60123 800-624-2926

Franklin Learning Resources, 122 Burrs Road, Mount Holly, NJ 08060 609-261-4800

GTE Educational Network Systems

   7566 Greenback Lane, Suite 801, Citrus Heights, CA 95610 .708-526-2682

Hartley, 9920 Pacific Heights Boulevard, Suite 500, San Diego, CA 92120 800-247-1380

Hi Tech for Blind Children 212-620-2020

Human Ware, Inc., 6245 King Road, Loomis, CA 95650 800-722-3393

IBM Special Needs, 1000 NW 51st Street, Boca Raton, FL 33432 407-982-9099

Infogrip, Inc., 1145 Engenia Place, Suite 201, Carpinteria, CA 93013 805-566-1049

IntelliTools, 5221 Central Avenue, Suite 205, Richmond, CA 94804 510-528-0670

Jouse, 1046 Deep Cove Road, North Vancouver, British Columbia V7V 153, Canada 604-929-2414

kidTECH, 21274 Oak Knoll, Tehachapi, CA 93561 805-822-1663

Laureate Learning Systems, 110 East Spring Street, Winooski, VT 05404 802-655-4755

Mayer-Johnson Co., P.O. Box 1579, Solana Beach, CA 92075 619-550-0084

National Geographic Society, Dept. 5413, Washington, DC 20039 800-368-2728

Nordic Software, 917 Carlos Drive, Lincoln, NE 68505-2059 .402-488-5086

Optimum Resource, Inc., 10 Station Place, Norfolk, CT 06058 800-327-1473

Recording for the Blind, 20 Roszel Road, Princeton, NJ 08540 609-520-8079

Tash Inc., 91 Station Street, #1, Ajax, Ontario L1S 3H2, Canada 905-686-4129

TeamRehab Report, 6133 Bristol Pkwy, Box 3640, Culver City, CA 90231 310-337-9717

Words+, P.O. Box 1229, Lancaster, CA 93584 800-869-8521

ASSISTIVE COMPUTER RESOURCES

When computers first became useful for the general population, it was assumed that everyone would be able to use the standard keyboard and, of course, that everyone would look at the monitor screen. In recent years, computer technology has spawned many pieces of specialized equipment and resources for the disabled. The field of telecommunications changes rapidly, and the resources listed were current at publication. Bulletin board systems and on-line services have been organized to assist the disabled.

Databases

• *ABLEDATA*   800-227-0216

This national database provides users with assistive technology information. It contains over 19,000 commercially available rehabilitation products and covers a wide array of topics.

• *NARIC (National Rehabilitation Information Center)* 800-277-0216 voice, TT•CO-NET available from Trace R and D Center   608-263-2309, voice 608-263-5408, TT

Cooperative Database Distribution Network for Assistive Technology is a CD-ROM disk that contains an electronic library. It includes the following: ABLEDATA database; REHABDATA database of publications and reports; Cooperative Service Directories database of services, service providers, and organizations; Publications, Media, and Materials database of publications and articles related to disability; and Text Document Library containing important documents related to disability and technology.

ASSISTIVE COMPUTER RESOURCES

Electronic Bulletin Boards of Interest to the Disabled

Many local, free bulletin board systems carry areas of interest to people with specific disabilities. These bulletin boards can be located by going on line with some of the numbers listed below, asking the system operator, or looking in computer-oriented newsletters and magazines.

Parents of the Visually Impaired (CA)	209-825-8537
BayTalk (Berkeley, CA)	415-864-6430
Body Dharma (Oakland, CA)	510-836-4717
CommunityInformationCenter (Rochester, NY)	716-293-2692
Disabled Children's Com. Group (Berkeley, CA)	510-841-5621
DEN-Disability Electronic NW (Hackensack, NJ)	210-342-3273
Department of Justice (Washington, DC)	202-514-6193
The Enabled Computer (Mahaffey, PA)	814-277-6337
SYNAPSE (Washington, DC)	202-543-9176
Handicap News (Bridgeport, CT)	303-337-1607
ADAnet (Birmingham, AL)	205-854-0698
Seattle Hearing (Seattle, WA)	206-526-2744
BrailleBank BBS (Croydon, PA)	215-244-9937
Information 90 BBS (Allentown, PA)	215-411-2237
JAN-Job Accommodation Network	800-342-5526
SpecialNeeds (Whiting, IN)	219-659-0112
HEX BBS (Baltimore, MD)	301-593-7357
National Federation of the Blind (Baltimore, MD)	301-752-5011
Nerd's Nook (Cleveland, OH)	216-356-1431
Black Bag BBS (Newark, DE)	302-731-1998
Denver Deaf Net BBS (Denver, CO)	303-989-9245
Project Enable (Dunbar, WV)	304-766-7842
Hearing Aid BBS (Miami, FL)	305-653-2589
Deaf Comm (Chicago, IL.)	612-262-6173
4Sights Network (Detroit, MI)	312-272-7111
Handiline (Fairfax, VA)	703-818-2660
DDConnection (Arlington, TX)	817-277-6989

ON-LINE COMPUTER SERVICES

Contact the following services by phone for the latest information on rates and access software.

America Online   800-827-6364

A special graphic-interface software is needed to log on. AOL will provide the disk on request through customer service. AOL has a disabilities area with messages in folders called Assistive Technology, Learning Disabilities, Deafness, Blindness, and Physically Disabled. An interactive session called the Equal Access Cafe is held monthly.

CompuServe   800-848-8199

The CompuServe graphic interface (CIM) makes the system easier to understand but does not work for those needing voice input or output. CompuServe can be connected to other communications software and will be text-based by default. CompuServe has a forum called Disabilities+ Forum. A message board and library are available.

DIMENET   508-880-5412

DIMENET is an on-line service promoting rights and independent living arrangements for the disabled. The network is well organized and consumer controlled. DIMENET stands for Disabled Individual's Movement for Equality Network.

GEnie   800-638-9636

GEnie is a consumer branch of General Electric's internal computer network and is text-based. It does not require special software.

Prodigy   800-776-3449

A basic fee gives users unlimited access to "core" services and limited access to "plus" services. The graphic interface provides an access barrier for some people with certain disabilities.

SeniorNet on America Online   415-750-5030

SeniorNet is an organization dedicated to computer-using seniors. Send e-mail to SeniorNet@AOL.com.

Tri-Star Computer   800-755-1000

Apple Computer operates the Applelink/E-World service. It requires a special graphic-interface software. A large collection of software and software demos can be downloaded, including adaptive technology. Empower Bulletin Board and other message areas are available.

WIDnet on Delphi   800-695-4005

Delphi is connected with the Internet, so users are able to access WIDnet in addition to Delphi and Internet. WIDnet provides electronic mail, on-line chat, conferencing, public discussions of policy issues, file libraries with ADA regulations, and other documents, as well as access to disability subject databases.

MEDIA AND VISUAL AIDS ON DISABILITIES

Media Distributors

Call or write these distributors to request catalogs.

Britannica Films, 310 South Michigan Avenue, Chicago IL 60604	800-554-9862
Campus Film Distributors, 24 Depot Square, Tuckahoe, NY 10707	800-BID-NET1
Captioned Films/Videos, 5000 Park Street N., St. Petersburg, FL 33709	800-237-6213
Coronet Films and Video, 108 Wilmot Road, Deerfield, IL 60015	800-777-8100
Council for Exceptional Children, 1920 Association Drive, Reston, VA 22091	703-620-3660
Direct Cinema Limited, P.O. 69799, Los Angeles, CA 90069-9976	213-656-4700
Great Plains National Instructional TV, University of Nebraska Box 80669, Lincoln, NE 68501	800-228-4630
Human Relations Media (HRM), 175 Tompkins Avenue, Pleasantville, NY 10570	800-431-2050
Mass Media Ministries, 2116 North Charles Street, Baltimore, MD 21218	301-727-3270
Media Guild, 11722 Sorrento Valley Road, Suite B, San Diego, CA 92121	619-755-9191
Modern Video Center, 5000 Park Street N., St. Petersburg, FL 33709	813-541-7571
PBS, P.O. Box 791, Alexandria, VA 22313-0791	800-328-7271
Research Press Co., Box 9177, Dept. N, Champaign, IL 61826	217-352-3273

Film and Video Recommendations

Like You, Like Me Series, from Britannica Films

This 10-program series is designed to help teachers and adults face the problems of integrating children with disabilities into their classrooms. The series consists of short stories about events in the lives of children who are disabled. An extended teacher's guide provides answers to many of the problems teachers may encounter. Each video is about six to seven minutes long and geared for kindergarten through primary grades. Preschool teachers need to view and evaluate the appropriateness of ideas for their classes.

Let's Talk It Over - a child with epilepsy
Let's Be Friends - a child who is emotionally disabled
Let Me Try - a child who is mentally impaired
Doing Things Together - a child with a prosthetic hand
Everyone Needs Some Help - a child with a speech and hearing impairment
See What I Feel - a child who is blind
When I Grow Up - career aspirations
Why Me? - a child with orthopedic disabilities
It's Up to Me - a child with asthma
I Can Do It - a child with double braces

OTHER FILM TITLES

Amy-on-the-Lips   32 minutes   Grades 4 - Adult   Coronet Films and Video
This is an adaptation from Disney's full-length feature, Amy. This program focuses on society's changing attitudes and the issues surrounding education for people with disabilities.

Autism   24 minutes   High School   Media Guild
This film explores two complementary areas of research in autism, one theoretical and one practical. Both focus on the autistic child's difficulty in understanding what people are thinking and feeling.

B Ball   28 minutes   Jr. High - Adults   Media Guild
A basketball team is formed with physically and mentally challenged players. This film is based on a book by the same title. The team, Wild Cats, is undefeated and has played against able-bodied teams and Special Olympic teams. Everyone wins in this film as the players challenge labels that have been attached to them, and self-esteem soars. It presents a view of family and job relationships.

Clockworks   16 minutes   Grades 7 - Adult   Coronet Films and Video
Misunderstood because he has Down syndrome, 12-year-old Scotty proves to be a capable assistant to a clock repairman. This film presents the idea that given a chance, those with mental challenges can function and contribute to our society.

Death: Coping with Loss   19 minutes   Grades 7 - Adult   Coronet Films and Video
People discuss fears about dying, responses to loss, the purpose of funerals, comforting the bereaved, and religious considerations of life after death.

Different Dance: Respecting Others   22 minutes   Grades 4 - 8   Coronet Films and Video
Eleven-year-old Maddy discovers her friend Lily's secret. Lily experiences taunting and humiliation from Maddy and the other girls. Ironically, by revealing her secret, her different culture, Lily is accepted by her classmates.

A Gift for Kate   28 minutes   Jr. High - Adult   Media Guild
Arthur's mother is discharged after 10 years in a mental institution and moves to a halfway house. The film depicts Arthur's growth in empathy and understanding for his mother's condition.

Give Me a Hand   17 minutes   All Levels   Britannica Films
This video presents the belief that there are no disabled people, just objects and environments inadequate for their needs.

Granpa   30 minutes   Preschool - Primary   Mass Media Ministries
This is an adaptation of the award-winning children's book by John Burningham that explores a special relationship between Emily and her grandfather. It deals with sensitive issues, including death.

OTHER FILM TITLES

The Hayburners   30 minutes   Grades 7 - Adult   Coronet Films and Video
   A 4-H contest is the setting for this film featuring a youngster named Will Bennett. Winning the contest with his "hayburner" seems impossible until Will meets up with a middle-aged, mentally impaired helper named Joe.

I'll Find a Way   26 minutes   All Levels   Media Guild
   Nadia was born with spina bifida, a malformation of the backbone that influences the development of the spinal cord and can cause crippling disabilities. This film, narrated by Nadia, provides viewers with important insights into how youngsters who are disabled function and how they'd like to be treated and thought of.

Just Like Anyone Else   30 minutes   Jr. High - Adult
   Strong young athletes play basketball in wheelchairs. These physically challenged young people speak and sign eloquently about their lives, their abilities, and their needs.

Just a Regular Kid: An AIDS Story   30 minutes   Jr. High - Adults   Media Guild
   A moving story of Kevin Casio, who was infected with the AIDS virus through a blood transfusion. This film depicts real-life experiences and shows how Kevin, his friends, and his family cope with sensitive issues.

Let's Talk about AIDS   14 minutes   Grades 3 - 6   HRM Video
   This film presents information about AIDS in a style appropriate for students in grades three through six. The film features peers, experts, and even kids with HIV.

Mirror, Mirror: A Story about Self-Respect   15 minutes   Grades 4 - 6   Coronet Films and Video
   Being bullied is an unpleasant situation, but for Josh Jacobson, a computer whiz, it's a way of life. Josh comes to understand that self-respect is a goal anyone can achieve — anyone willing to work for it.

My Friends Call Me Tony   12 minutes   Kindergarten - Adults   Media Guild
   Tony became blind after an operation to remove a brain tumor at the age of three. Now he is ten and is learning to live a full and fulfilling life despite his "disability."

Regina: Gift of Vision   11 minutes   All levels   Britannica Films
   The everyday experiences of a person with a disability are shared by 11-year-old Regina.

Rick, You're In   20 minutes   Grades 7 - Adult   Disney Educational Productions
   This story about mainstreaming provides insights into the problems, triumphs, and frustrations of people with disabilities, as well as the aspirations and interests they enjoy.

OTHER FILM TITLES

A Victory of the Spirit   56 minutes   Jr. High - Adult   HRM Video

This film is an extraordinary documentary featuring two young North Carolina Special Olympians. It shows the reality of mental impairment and the everyday challenges and victories that these two young men experience.

Yours to Keep   72 minutes   General Audience   Direct Cinema Limited

This film stars John Taylor, an engaging, ambitious teenager who happens to have Down syndrome. It portrays the tale of an extraordinary young man who must come to terms with society's limited expectations of him. He has an encyclopedic memory for music history and dreams of becoming a disk jockey.

Truly Exceptional People

Dan Haley   11 minutes   Grades 4 - 12   Coronet Films and Video

Dan Haley faces life totally blind, but he is anything but helpless. After spending time with Dan, viewers will have a clear sense of individual human potential.

Joni   75 minutes   General Audience   Mass Media Ministries

Joni was just 17 when a diving accident left her paralyzed and in a wheelchair. Joni Eareckson Tada stars as herself in this powerful film adaptation of her best-selling autobiography.

Terry Fox: The Power of Purpose   24 minutes   Jr. High - Adult   Mass Media Ministries

This is the story of Terry Fox, the Canadian teenager who lost a leg to cancer but responded to his personal tragedy by running across Canada to raise money for cancer research. Motivational and uplifting.

Tom and Virl Osmond   15 minutes   Grades 4 - 12   Coronet Films and Video

This story of the two older Osmond brothers is an inspiration to students with speech and hearing disabilities.

Factual Information Films from Britannica Films

Learning to Use Your Senses   9 minutes   Primary Level
Your Ears 9 minutes   Primary Level
Your Eyes 9 minutes   Primary Level
For facilitators, teachers, and parents

OTHER FILM TITLES

Many valuable films and videos are produced on special needs topics that interest kids. The titles are too numerous to list here. Write or call the following companies for more information about what is currently available.

- *Captioned Films/Videos Modern Talking Picture Service, Inc.*
  5000 Park Street N., St. Petersburg, FL 33709

  This company provides free loan of educational and general interest films and videos. The program is made available by the U.S. Department of Education, Office of Special Education. Users of 16-mm films are required to pay return postage. One-half-inch VHS videos with prepaid return postage labels included in the cassette cases are free to use. An application process must be completed prior to use. Request applications and brochures from the company.

- *The Council for Exceptional Children*, Dept. K4012, 1920 Association Drive, Reston, VA 22091-1589

- *Films for the Humanities and Sciences*, P.O. Box 2053, Princeton, NJ 08543-2053
  Subjects include psychology, mental health, and health.

- *GPN*, P.O. Box 80669, Lincoln, NE 68501
  A comprehensive catalog for all subject areas.

- *Kid Love Unlimited*, 2973 Harbor Blvd., #508, Costa Mesa, CA 92626
  A potpourri of materials on awareness and the appreciation of learning differences. A must-see film for everyone!

OTHER FILM TITLES

How Difficult Can This Be?   70 minutes   All Ages
Frustration, Anxiety, and Tension
   This moving video gives an excellent view of what it's like to be a learner with disabilities. Each of us has some form of learning disability which may be mild or severe. This video builds awareness and empathy for all learning differences.
       Available from PBS — 800-328-7271
       For home use, order copy number HDFF-000WSW $39.95
       For school or educational use, order copy number HDFF-901WSW $49.95
       To purchase in bulk, call 1-800-344-3337

Take a Giant Step   30 minutes   Adults   Campus Film Distributors Corp.
   This film uses live action and narration to show how play can be used therapeutically in schools, hospitals, institutions, group homes, day care, child development centers, and community programs that care for the disabled.

Special Children, Different Needs   30 minutes   Adults   Campus Film Distributors Corp.
   This film continues to follow the seven children highlighted in *Special Children, Special Needs*. This new film documents the current status and changes that have taken place in the children, their parents, and the school staffs.

Special Children, Special Needs   22 minutes   Adults   Campus Film Distributors Corp.
   This film presents a comprehensive approach to educating young children with disabilities. Three adapted learning environments are featured: an infant setting, a preschool learning laboratory, and an outdoor therapeutic playground.

Parenting Children with Disabilities   30 minutes   Adults   Research Press Co.
   This video focuses on critical issues such as the birth and diagnosis of a child with disabilities, the impact on the family system, psychological stages that most parents of children with disabilities will experience, review of special education laws, and the importance of early intervention.

Parents' View of Living With a Child With Disabilities   30 minutes   Adults   Research Press Co.
   This video features in-depth, candid interviews in which parents of children with disabilities share their personal concerns and experiences. Difficulties and dilemmas in dealing with the health care profession are highlighted.

THE TWO OF US BENEATH THE LARGE, OLD TREE

I lived in a neighborhood with very few kids,
so one day as I was walking past a stone house
and I saw you playing behind a large, old tree,
oh, how the sight of you excited me.
I shouted, "Hey, let's play."
      You stared back at me
      with eyes so big and round –
      and then you just sat down
      beneath that large, old tree.
      You didn't even say "Hi" back to me.

The next morning on my walk,
there you were playing behind that large, old tree.
I shouted, "Hey, let's have some fun together today."
      You stared back at me
      with eyes so big and round –
      and then you just sat down
      beneath that large, old tree.
      You didn't even talk to me.

A few days later as I walked past your stone house,
I saw you again playing behind that large, old tree.
I was tired of feeling left out
so I just waved in passing.
      You burst into a smile and waved back to me.
      I ran right to you and blurted out, "What do you want to play?"
      You stared back at me
      with eyes so big and round –
      then you just sat down and so I sat down,
      and there the two of us were sitting together,
      just you and me beneath that large, old tree.

"Hello," I said feeling awkward.
"Ollo," you said back strangely.
Then you grabbed my hands and pressed them up against my ears.
Suddenly I couldn't hear. Everything was just quiet.
I looked into your eyes so big and round –
and knew you and I were different in our world of sound.

     You took my right hand and pressed it against your chest.
     I felt the beating of your heart.
     You took my other hand and pressed it against my chest.
     I felt the beating of my heart.
     With my two hands you said, "We are the same.
     We both can love with a heart."

We jumped up and played all day until the sun set.
We played in fall leaves and in the cold winter wind,
we played while spring birds built their nest,
and we played and hid from the summer sun
beneath that large, old tree after we met.

As we grew, you taught me to slow down,
to hear the quiet sounds,
to hear my heart speak.
And my dear friend,
my life could not have been ever complete
without you in my world.

—Jeanne Maree Iacono

MEET THE AUTHORS AND ILLUSTRATOR

Dee Konczal has been active in education since 1963 as a classroom teacher and a teacher of the visually impaired. She is currently an Assistive Technology Specialist at Ventura Community College. She is a member of Pi Lambda Theta and the California Association of Post Secondary Education for the Disabled. She has been an active volunteer for many groups, including Girl Scouts, Boy Scouts, Ventura County Braille Transcribers Association, and the Retinitis Pigmentosa Association of Ventura County, as well as a high school church counselor. She loves collecting antiques, reading, gardening, and spending time at her family's mountain retreat.

Veronica Getskow has taught preschool, kindergarten, and early childhood classes at the community college and university levels. Currently she is working on a doctorate at UCLA Graduate School of Education. She is a member of Delta Kappa Gamma, Pi Lambda Theta, the National Association for the Education of Young Children, and the Southern California Kindergarten Conference Board. She enjoys adding to a collection of silver tree ornaments and continuing her quest to own all of the Caldecott Award-winning books.

Bev Armstrong graduated with honors from the Art Center College of Design. When not at the drawing board, she enjoys being with people—visiting nursing homes, working as a camp counselor, teaching humane society classes, helping with Special Olympics, and training church members to help people in crisis. Bev is a little person whose size has not stopped her from doing much of anything. She shares her home with more than fifty pets.